ISSUES IN ASSESSMENT AND TESTING

Series Editors: Donald McLeod and Ingrid Lunt

UNDERSTANDING PSYCHOLOGICAL TESTING

Charles Jackson

Institute for Employment Studies

BPS
BOOKS

Published by The British Psychological Society

First published in 1996 by BPS Books (The British Psychological Society)
St Andrews House, 48 Princess Road East, Leicester LE1 7DR, UK.

A catalogue record for this book is available from the British Library.

ISBN 1 85433 200 7

Set in Montotype Baskerville by Patrick Armstrong, Book Production
Services, 28a Grove Vale, London SE22 8DY

Printed and bound in Great Britain by
Biddles Ltd, Guildford and King's Lynn

Contents

List of figures

Issues in assessment and testing

Psychological testing has been around for a long time. It is here to stay, and the use of tests in some form or another is going to continue to expand. So what is it all about? That is one of the questions that we are setting out to try to answer in this series. And at whom is it aimed? Anyone who is at all interested in finding out about tests and other forms of psychological assessment, for whatever reason.

For almost the whole of the twentieth century psychologists have been devising ways of assessing all manner of human attributes – feelings and fears, skills and aptitudes, beliefs and attitudes, wants and needs, insights and interests. Their quest has had two main aims. One, the theoretical, has been the advancement of knowledge about the psychology of the human species. The other, the practical, is about finding ways of helping to put that knowledge into effect. Our interest focuses in large measure on the latter, the principles-into-practice side, but not so intently as to exclude some of the more interesting theoretical and philosophical issues that surround and underpin psychological assessment.

Assessment in some shape or form pervades just about everything that we do. Formally or informally, we find assessments being made during the course of our education, in our working lives, when we get ill, and even if and when we offend against society's codes of behaviour. Children are assessed in a variety of ways, ideally – though maybe not always – as a means of ensuring that their development follows its most effective path to the full development of their individual capabilities. Young people and adults are assessed for their suitability for a particular line of work or for their potential to develop into it. People in work are increasingly involved in assessment for career development purposes, for promotion, for succession planning, for the purposes of putting together effective working teams, and so on. If our mental health falters, there will be assessments aimed at finding ways of helping us back to a state where we are at the very least better able to cope. Those who offend against the law may on occasion be assessed to determine their fitness to plead, and assessment will form an integral part of any programme of rehabilitation for the inmates of our prisons. It is all around us, and psychological testing is one of the forms that it typically takes.

Tests come in an extraordinarily wide array of forms, styles, content and purpose. But underneath it all there are really only two main kinds. One of them centres on ability – on knowledge, skills and aptitudes. The focus of the other is on our 'personality' – what kind of people we are, how we typically respond to the world around us and how we make that world respond to us. Although the technical terms 'psychometrics' or 'psychometric test' are often used, they imply nothing more than 'psychological test' – the term that we will use throughout the series.

There is already a great deal in print that is aimed at the specialist, at the testing and assessment professional. *Issues in Assessment and Testing* is not that kind of series. It does not set out to compete with specialist volumes in test construction. Rather, its aim is to try to meet the needs of the 'lay' practitioner, or of the interested observer with a healthy but unmet interest in the issues that surround psychological assessment and testing. We aim not so much to promote psychological testing and assessment as to help shed as much light as possible on the whole area. We hope to open up discussion, to enhance understanding of what tests and other formal assessment methods can achieve, and to foster a better educated use of methods and procedures of these sorts.

In this first book in the series, Charles Jackson lays out the groundwork. In essence he tells us how tests and testing work. He writes for the person who, without being a test specialist or a professional in the field, is nevertheless involved in some way in the use of psychological testing – or who might become involved in it. This applies, of course, not only to the user of tests but to those who find themselves being assessed, and he includes an extremely helpful 'Guide for test takers' as an appendix to the main text. But he also writes for the person who simply wants to know more about it, for no reason other than pure interest. For the sake of clarity and simplicity, he focuses in the main on the use of testing in employment settings – selection for recruitment, for career counselling and development, and so on – with occasional reference to educational usage. The more clinical uses are not addressed in any depth, his aim being to use examples from employment as a means of explaining the principles and practice that underlie all psychological testing, for whatever purpose.

One theme comes through strongly and is worthy of endorsement. Assessment and testing was once seen largely as a one-way process, when the expert tested, deliberated and pronounced with almost no further involvement on the participant's part than to sit there and take the test. That can no longer hold. To a greater or lesser extent, psychological assessment and testing has become an enterprise where the involvement and the rights of both parties, assessee as much as assessor, are out in the open. It has now to be seen as a two-way participative process, which emphasizes once again the value that we hope this book, and future books in the series, will have not only for those who use such procedures, but for those who are assessed by them too.

Donald McLeod and Ingrid Lunt
Series Editors

Preface

The development and use of psychological tests is probably what psychology is best known for to the world at large. Over the last ten years or so, the impact of testing in the UK has increased considerably and more people are affected by testing than ever before. This book aims to introduce people to the process of psychological testing. It assumes little or no prior knowledge of the purposes for which testing is used or of the range of situations where tests have been found to be useful.

Frequently, psychological testing is only considered from the perspective of the person administering the test or the user of the test results (not always the same person). In this book, considerable attention is also given to the person who takes the test – the test taker. All test use should promote the test taker's self-understanding. Users of tests need to be aware how the process of testing itself can influence test performance and how the context in which tests are used can affect the person taking a test.

The proper use of tests can promote fairness and equality of opportunity. This means at the very least that test takers participate in testing on the basis of informed consent and are given feedback on their test performance. It also means that users of tests recognize their professional and ethical responsibilities and are aware of the inherent limitations of testing, as well as its strengths.

Any technical subject generates its own specialized vocabulary, its jargon terms. Psychological testing is no different, and for this reason I have included a glossary at the back of the book that gives the meaning of key terms. When one of these terms is first used in the text, it is printed in bold.

I have also included a short technical appendix showing how to calculate percentile and standard scores and a listing of sources of further information. This includes a guide for further reading, sources of test reviews, contact addresses for two test user groups and the addresses of relevant professional organizations.

As most of us are more likely to be asked to take a test than to administer one, there is also a short guide for test takers. This has been written jointly with Ann Turner and is based on an earlier guide we wrote for the University of Wales Careers Service in Cardiff. This is a short summary of many of the issues involved in taking tests which are discussed in greater detail in the main text. It also includes some example test questions.

What I have learnt about psychological testing has come from many sources. However, I am particularly indebted to Geoff Brown, who first introduced me to the use of psychological tests when I was a postgraduate student, and to René Dawis, who over the years has always been most generous with his time and knowledge. I am also extremely grateful to Peter Herriot and Ann Turner for their extensive and helpful comments on the first draft. I would also like to thank all those who have supplied me with material for figures or other essential information.

Charles Jackson
February, 1996
Brighton

Note: No reference to specific, commercially available tests in this book may be taken as implying that the BPS endorses the instrument in question. The BPS endorses neither test publishers nor their products.

1 Why is it important to know about psychological tests?

Psychological testing is often in the news but not all the publicity is good. When Anglian Water in the UK employed consultants to assess their staff prior to announcing large-scale redundancies, it gave rise to headlines like: 'Question: Do you want to be fired?' (*Daily Mail*, June 8, 1994), 'Cult of the personality test' (The *Observer*, October 9, 1994). The assessment exercise had included completing a personality questionnaire and the newspapers were incensed that this seemed to form the basis for choosing who was to be made redundant, although this was subsequently denied by Alan Smith, Anglian Water's Managing Director (The *Observer*, October 16, 1994).

However, cases like this give rise to many questions. For example:

- Can personality questionnaires be used to predict future job performance?

- Do some of the questions amount to an invasion of privacy when used in this context?

- What would happen if people refused to participate in such an exercise?

- Were the consultants and the company acting ethically towards their staff in conducting such an exercise?

- Should previous work performance have been considered in deciding who to make redundant?

Despite the fact that the Anglian Water case related only to the use of one test in one situation, such publicity is damaging to the way people think about psychological tests and the testing process. The issue at Anglian Water was whether it was appropriate to use a particular type of psychological **test**; whether an organization should treat its employees in this way; what rights employees have when they are asked to take tests.

As Cronbach (1975) notes: 'Sound policy is not for tests or against tests; what matters is how tests are used.' In real life it is not always easy to distinguish between the two, so tests get blamed and testing as a whole is tarnished by association.

Unfortunately, there are other examples of psychological tests being used in controversial ways. For example, is it appropriate to use tests to screen job applicants for sales positions for predisposition to steal or pilfer? To what extent should the content of a test administered at the end of an education or training course be allowed to shape what is taught? No doubt the reader can think of more examples where the use of tests or the way that test results are used should be questioned.

Problems may arise from technical issues affecting the use of a particular test in a certain situation, but of more concern is the fact that test use may raise ethical issues. For example, is it ever appropriate: to use deception about the purpose of testing; to judge people as potentially guilty when they have done nothing wrong; to invade an individual's privacy; to ask people to testify against themselves. And in cases where children are tested, what rights do their parents have to information about the test results?

In the United States many controversial testing practices have been challenged in the courts. For example, the use of one personality measure by an employer was judged inappropriate because the content was not clearly job-related. There has also been considerable controversy in the United States about testing policies that allocated a high proportion of black children to special education classes. (This debate echoes many of the issues associated with the use of the eleven-plus in the UK – see Chapter 2.) In Britain as well there have been legal challenges to the use of tests in some circumstances, particularly in employment settings.

Key social and ethical issues for testing practice concern gaining informed consent for participation in the testing process, respecting the confidentiality of the person being tested and communicating test results properly. The underlying ethic is that the dignity of the person being tested must be respected. Providing this is achieved, the proper use of tests can promote fairness and equality of opportunity. On the other hand, inappropriate use of tests or inadequate testing processes can lead to bias and unfair discrimination against some candidates.

Increased use of tests

One reason why there is an increasing level of concern about how psychological tests are being used is that their use is becoming more widespread. In part this is because psychology is having a greater impact on many aspects of life. Every year psychologists are responsible for the administration of millions of tests in a wide variety of settings, including the workplace, educational institutions, hospitals and clinics as well as in career and counselling services. At one time administering tests was probably the main activity of those psychologists who were not involved in teaching and research. Nowadays the majority of psychologists probably spend only a small proportion, if any, of their time in psychological testing. However, there are many more psychologists now than in the past. For example, in 1995 The British Psychological Society (BPS) had 19,443 members compared with only 3,811 in 1970, so that in 25 years membership has increased approximately five times. Of the current members, over 8,500 are registered as Chartered Psychologists with Practising Certificates and can be considered to be working as professional psychologists.

Furthermore, many non-psychologists have been trained to use tests and they now probably administer more tests than do psychologists. Currently there are over 7,400 non-members of the BPS holding a Level A Statement or Certificate of Competence in Occupational Testing compared with about 1,500 members. Others who administer tests include schoolteachers, careers advisers and speech therapists.

However, the main reason why the use of psychological tests has become more widespread is that they are perceived to be useful. In a wide variety of situations, ranging from selecting people for jobs, to assisting people to make educational and career decisions, there is evidence that decisions made on the basis of test results, either alone or in conjunction with other information, have more positive outcomes than decisions made without information from tests. We will review this evidence in greater detail in the next chapter 'Why use tests?' because it is obviously crucial to any understanding of psychological testing.

We have all taken tests

One important consequence of this growth in the amount of psychological testing taking place is that nearly everyone in industrialized societies has completed a psychological test at some point in their lives. For example, having to complete or 'take' a test is a regular occurrence in schools, so most children will complete a psychological test at some point in their education. Increasingly, tests are also being used in employment settings, for selecting people for jobs, for instance. This means that psychological tests and psychological testing are one of the most visible of all psychology's enterprises. For this reason alone, there is a need for more people to have a basic understanding of what is involved in using psychological tests:

- the underlying assumptions of testing
- the different sorts of psychological tests
- the various purposes for which tests are used
- how test scores should be interpreted
- where it is possible to find out more about tests.

The purpose of this book is to answer some of these most basic questions about psychological testing. Reading this book will not give anyone the skills required to use tests themselves, although it will make clear what is required for competent test use, and will explain how people should acquire these skills.

Using test results

This book is also aimed at those who *use* test results. Many more people are nowadays presented with the results of psychological testing, which could be test scores, computer-generated narrative reports or reports written by the person who interpreted the test, than administer and interpret the tests themselves. Potential consumers of the results of psychological testing include not only the person who has taken the test but also many other interested parties. In schools it includes teachers who might be making educational decisions on the basis of pupils' test results; in the world of work it includes managers and employers who might be making decisions on whether to recruit someone for a job, on who to promote, or send on a training course, and so on.

Even excluding those who take psychological tests, the number of users of test results is much greater than the number of people who administer tests. While it is primarily the responsibility of the person who is interpreting the test results to inform other users of the appropriate ways that the results might be interpreted, it is virtually impossible for these second-level users to be critical consumers without some understanding of psychological testing. This book is written with this wider audience also in mind.

Best practice suggests that when people take tests they should always be given some feedback on their test performance. Unfortunately in the past this was rarely the case and probably most people who have taken tests have been given no feedback on their test performance. This may be one reason why psychological tests are frequently viewed with suspicion and distrust.

We all now expect to be told more about matters that affect us. Society is more open; information is more widely available. Politicians and others argue for freedom of information, even if they do not always put into practice what they preach. In the past, professionals such as doctors and lawyers were perceived as experts whose opinions and judgements were not open to question. Psychologists' use of tests was no different and so they were not concerned with explaining themselves and their professional techniques to the wider audience. However, testing practice is changing and giving feedback should be the norm. The issue of how to give appropriate feedback is discussed in Chapter 7 'How to use tests properly.'

Knowing more about testing

Many people just want to know more about psychological testing. This is a short introductory book that assumes no prior knowledge but aims to explain in a straightforward manner how psychological tests are used. Issues to do with testing are often related to matters of public policy or concern. The debate about the role of assessment in schools, for example, is about the content of the tests, the appropriateness of testing at particular ages and how the results of testing should be used. While this book cannot claim to offer definitive answers, it does aim to explore some of the underlying assumptions in testing and so contribute to informing the discussion on issues to do with the use of tests.

Debates about the appropriateness of the use of tests in particular situations frequently involve more than consideration of the technical merits of a particular test. They often also include discussion of more underlying issues; for example, the process of intellectual development, or psychologists' evolving ideas about intellectual ability. While detailed consideration of such issues is beyond the scope of this book, they can have important implications for testing programmes.

Tests versus testing

Psychological testing can be described as the process of using psychological tests. It sounds so simple – the test exists; instructions are followed; the test is administered, scored and interpreted; testing has taken place.

If only testing were a simple mechanical process, it would be straightforward; in practice it is more complicated. Candidates need to be put at ease about the purpose of testing; they will want to ask questions if they do not understand the instructions; they may be affected by the **style** or manner of the test administrator. Furthermore, test scores cannot be interpreted without an understanding of key measurement and technical issues.

There is limited value, therefore, in discussing tests without considering how they are used. Of course, psychologists and others do talk about tests, reviews of tests are published, test suppliers market tests, but all these processes assume that the tests will be used appropriately. Understanding psychological testing means knowing how to use tests in an appropriate manner. It also means being aware of the assumptions that underpin the development and use of tests, and how these have changed over time.

Even psychologists who do not use tests need to know about these issues because so much psychological knowledge is based on data from tests. The measurement principles on which testing is based also have implications for much psychological research that does not itself use standardized measures. Questionnaire-based measures are widely used in survey research. Such research might include, for example, surveys to examine employee morale or market research studies investigating aspects of consumer behaviour. Questionnaires are also frequently used by psychologists in laboratory-based research, to measure subjects' attitudes or knowledge, for example. In these circumstances, it is just as important that the measurement processes, such as the questionnaires used in surveys, produce data that measure as accurately as possible what is intended.

One of the objectives of this book is to make clearer the issues and measurement principles involved in evaluating the ways that tests are used. This means making people aware of the issues involved in giving an appropriate test interpretation and in using test results. The focus is on finding out what you need to know to use tests. This includes where to find out about tests, how to use key reference sources, scoring procedures, and the issues involved in communicating test results. The book does not provide a compilation of test reviews, although it does include brief descriptions of a few tests. This has been done primarily to illustrate the range of tests available and the various approaches to test design. Sources of further information about specific tests are listed at the end of the book.

Other forms of assessment

Psychological testing is only one way of assessing people. However, many of the principles that underpin psychological testing are also directly relevant to other methods of assessment, such as interviewing. For example, all measurement procedures have a degree of error associated with them and consequently need to be evaluated to see whether they yield consistent results. All measurement is carried out for a reason and the value of any assessment method can be judged by how well it meets its stated purpose. Similarly, there are assumptions built into any measurement procedure about what is being assessed. How such issues affect psychological testing has been studied in great detail and, as a result, it is possible to generalize to other methods of assessment many of the insights that have been gained from the research done on tests and testing.

One setting where tests are often used alongside other forms of assessment is the **assessment centre.** Assessment centres are frequently used as part of the employment selection process. The assessment centre, which has become increasingly popular as a way of assessing people in organizations, relies on the notion that assessment using a variety of different methods, for example role plays, interviews and group discussions, as well as tests, is likely to give a better overall picture of the candidate's strengths and weaknesses than any single assessment technique on its own. By being more comprehensive in its approach, the assessment centre would seem intuitively to be fairer to candidates, although whether this is always the case in practice may be open to debate. In reality, the evaluation of any particular assessment technique needs to demonstrate that:

- the procedure has been well designed

- it has been appropriately administered

- any information generated from it has been interpreted correctly

- appropriate decisions have been made on the basis of it.

The processes which psychologists use to evaluate assessment methods have evolved from the methods developed for evaluating psychological tests that are described in this book.

The main participants

Tests are used by people. It is important, therefore, to identify the various roles of the participants in the testing process. Participants can be divided into those who are directly involved in a particular testing session and those who are associated with the testing process more indirectly, although their role may be equally important. Sometimes one individual assumes more than one of these roles.

Direct participants in the testing process are:

Test user: the person who requires the test results, normally for some decision-making purpose. Sometimes this person provides scores or test interpretations to someone else who has, or shares, decision-making responsibilities. For example, if the test user is supplying results to an employer, both are test users and they share responsibility for ensuring proper test use.

Test taker: the individual who takes the test by choice, direction or necessity. In some cases this individual is also the ultimate consumer (e.g. in careers counselling), where an individual not only takes the test but is also the main user of the test results. In such circumstances special care is needed to provide an appropriate context for understanding the test results.

Test administrator: the person who supervises and has responsibility for administering the test. If test administration is either delegated to another person or delivered by a computer, the test administrator is the person who can be considered responsible for ensuring adherence to sound professional practice.

Second level participants are:

Test developer: the person or group of people who develop, publish and market the test. The development role is sometimes split between the following:

 Test author: the person who originally develops and researches the test.

 Test publisher: the organization which markets and distributes the test and its accompanying documentation, such as the **test manual**, scoring keys and so on, which are required to use a test. The test publisher sometimes also provides scoring services.

 Software author: the person who develops the computer programs that administer, score and sometimes provide an interpretation of the test.

 Test sponsor: usually an organization (employer, government agency or other public body) that contracts for the development of the test or the provision of the testing service.

Test reviewer: the person who conducts a scholarly review to evaluate the suitability of the test for its proposed uses.

This book is targeted primarily at the direct users of tests – the test user, the test taker and the test administrator. However, with its emphasis on test use, the book may also be of interest to people in organizations that sponsor such use. We also hope that discussion of the way tests are used will be of interest to those who are normally more concerned with the technical issues of test development, although they clearly have their own specialist texts to refer to.

Concerns about testing

As the use of tests increases, the range of concerns about testing widens. Three issues that particularly affect the way tests are used are discussed below.

The impact of computers might be thought of as primarily a technical issue but it has many implications for test use as well. How to improve test use is a major concern of all of us who believe that using tests appropriately has significant benefits. The misuse of any test damages the credibility of all test use. All users and potential users of tests should be concerned to promote the better use of tests.

If psychologists have learnt anything about using tests, it is the need to be aware of the context in which tests are being used if test results are to be interpreted appropriately. Some applications of tests will always be controversial; there is always a need to consider the social and ethical issues involved in using tests.

The impact of computers

Although there is a trend for tests to be revised more frequently, the underlying principles of test use evolve more slowly. However, over the last ten years the continued impact of computers has changed many aspects of testing. Many tests are now administered via computer. Old tests have been converted for administration by computer and new ones developed to take advantage of special features that become possible when computers are used, for example dynamic displays in contrast to static line drawings.

The use of computers for **ability** and **aptitude tests** has permitted the development of what are called '**adaptive**' tests where tests are tailored to the individual. Here the answer that a person gives to one question affects the next question the person is asked.

In other settings, the increased use of computers has led to the development of more sophisticated scoring procedures. In the case of many personality questionnaires, computer-generated narrative reports have been developed where a computer program prints a report that interprets an individual's test scores. As the interpretation of measures of personality has always been a complex task, the availability of these reports has probably meant that more people want to use these measures.

The implications of the use of computers and other recent technical developments in testing are discussed in Chapter 3 'What is a psychological test?'

Improving test use

As the use of tests has grown, so too have concerns about test use. These concerns can take many forms. There is misuse of tests, where tests are used in situations for which they were not designed or where the test scores will not contribute to the assessment decision. There are poorly designed tests and even situations in which tests have been published but where the test scores are meaningless. There is considerable concern about fairness in testing and whether tests can be biased against certain groups. These concerns will be discussed in Chapter 6 'How to judge tests' and Chapter 7 'How to use tests properly'.

A major reason for inappropriate test use is lack of training. Unfortunately perhaps, there is no 'big brother' supervising all test use or all test sales. Tests do fall into the hands of people who are not trained to use them. In a limited number of situations it may be correct to criticize the test, but much more often it is not the test but rather the use to which it is being put that is at fault. Although it is the test user who should be blamed, all too often it is the test (and tests and testing in general) that suffers.

One major aim of this book is to convince potential test users of the need for training before they use tests. Chapter 9 discusses these issues and outlines both the general issues involved and current practice in the UK for obtaining training and becoming registered with a test publisher as a qualified test user. In recent years the professional organizations concerned with the use of tests in Britain, including The British Psychological Society (BPS) and the Institute of Personnel and Development (IPD), as well as the major test publishers, have launched a number of initiatives to encourage people to seek training before they use tests, and to regulate the use of tests by their members through professional accreditation procedures.

Testing in context

Testing cannot be considered in isolation. Test scores can only be understood in relation to other known facts about the individual. Scores themselves are only estimates and not fixed immutable characteristics of people. One key issue to remember is that psychologists' own theories and understanding of what test performance means have been evolving, as have psychologists' theoretical concepts of, for example, what intelligence means. This is one way that context has affected testing.

There is also a greater awareness of how social and cultural factors affect test performance and the influence this should have on the meaning that can be attributed to test scores. Tests cannot be culture free and there are no generic tests appropriate for all situations. Rather there is a need to be clearer about the specific contexts and purposes for which a particular test has been designed. Becoming a test user involves being aware of how these issues can affect the choice of test for a particular situation. Factors that can lead to inappropriate test use are discussed in Chapter 6 'How to judge tests'.

Summary

Psychological tests are more widely used now than at any time in the past. However, the increased use of tests has not been without controversy. There is, therefore, a continuing need for people to be better informed about psychological testing, its advantages and disadvantages. Nearly all of us have completed a test at some point in our lives. Many of us are also consumers of test results, for example as managers responsible for selecting people for jobs, as parents or teachers of children who take tests as part of their education.

This chapter has reviewed some important changes in the ways that tests are being used. These include both technical developments, for example the variety of ways in which computers are influencing testing practice, and changes in social expectations which have resulted in it becoming the norm for people to receive feedback on their test performance. There is also greater awareness of the effects of social and cultural factors on testing.

The book is about testing, that is how tests are used. It aims to help people understand what can be considered an appropriate use for a particular test and to identify potential pitfalls when using tests.

2 Why use tests?

One of the most obvious things about people is that they are all different. This is not just true in terms of physical characteristics such as height, colour of eyes and hair, gender and so on, but also in other ways. We differ in our abilities, our strengths and weaknesses, the way we behave, what we like and dislike. Note that even so-called identical twins may be genetically identical but variations in their environmental experiences lead to differences between them.

Our uniqueness is something to celebrate. Not only would it be very boring if we were all the same, or even if only some of us were identical to each other, but it also would limit our ability to change and adapt. Diversity, which is the basis of natural selection, is therefore an important asset.

While recognizing our individual uniqueness, we also realize that as human beings we all have certain things in common: we all breathe and walk upright, for example. These characteristics are what identify us as a species. Between these two extremes, we recognize that each individual shares things in common with some individuals but not with others. This is readily apparent in terms of physical characteristics such as eye colour, height, shoe size but is also true of other characteristics, our preferences for different activities, our skills and so on.

It was this recognition that there are similarities as well as differences between people and, what is more, that such similarities and differences can have important practical consequences, that led to the study of individual differences becoming an important part of psychology. However, the development of any science is critically dependent on the availability of suitable measurement procedures. The psychological test embodies those measurement procedures and its development revolutionized psychological science. The invention and subsequent development of psychological tests is 'comparable in its impact to the telescope in physics and the microscope in biology' (Dawis, 1992).

So the first answer to the question, 'Why use tests?' is that tests are one of the main measurement tools that psychologists have developed to study differences between people. If you are interested in how people differ, you need to know about psychological tests.

But why should anyone be interested in the differences between people? The answer here is straightforward. It is because these differences have direct and practical consequences for all of us in our lives. Understanding the ways in which people differ enables a wide range of questions to be addressed. For example:

- What jobs would I be good at?

- Which job applicant should be employed?

- What subjects should I study at school/college?

- Who will benefit from this training programme?

- Which children need compensatory education?

- How can my interpersonal skills be improved?

While some of these questions primarily concern individuals and others organizations or society at large, all are concerned with making predictions. As soon as it is recognized that differences between people exist and that life offers choices, there is a natural interest in trying to predict which one of two or more situations will lead to the best outcome. For the employer, the desired outcome is to choose the best applicant for the job; for the school or college student it is to choose the most appropriate subjects to study; for the school it is to ensure that the children who need compensatory or special education receive it. Such decisions are an inevitable part of life in contemporary society.

Once it has been recognized that making decisions involves making a prediction about the future, the issue then becomes one about the information that should be used in the decision-making process. The reasons for considering the use of tests to generate information to help us make our decisions in a more rational way are that tests are relatively efficient in terms of time and money, and produce high quality information. (For a discussion of the irrational nature of much human decision-making, see Sutherland, 1994.)

Although it may take a great deal of time, money and effort to construct and develop a psychological test, in the long run using a standardized test is usually more economical of time and money than more subjective methods of assessment. The benefits of using psychological tests therefore outweigh the costs of developing and using them. Furthermore, psychological tests provide standardized techniques and procedures. These are fairer to people than the traditional impressionistic techniques, which are vulnerable to prejudice and bias on the part of the assessor. However, tests share some limitations with other assessment techniques. For example, any assessment process can only measure performance or preferences at a particular moment in time. People do change and, as will be stressed throughout this book, the interpretation of the results of tests or other assessment techniques should always take into account the context (both time and situation) in which the assessment has taken place.

Studying differences between people

We make two main assumptions when we study people:

- characteristics of people are measurable
- differences between people are of interest.

Developing an understanding of how people differ has underpinned the application of psychology in many areas because it has offered useful techniques for solving real problems. This is because of the measurement principles and measurement techniques that have been developed and embodied in psychological tests. This measurement technology underpins psychological assessment in many other applied settings.

Many applied situations are inherently complex. They are settings where many factors can be considered to be affecting how people behave. In technical terms, such situations are **multivariate**. Much scientific work carried out in these circumstances attempts to clarify already existing relationships. For example, someone studying the extent to which educational **attainment** might influence job performance has to take account of many other factors, such as motivation, age, health and so on, that might also affect someone's performance of their job. A significant achievement of applied psychology has been the development of techniques for analysing these situations.

This approach can be distinguished from the experimental approach which often studies behaviour in artificial settings (e.g. laboratories), where only one or two **variables** are manipulated to assess their impact on subjects' behaviour.

Modern psychological science draws on both of these research traditions and much contemporary research explores interactions between them. Increasingly, it is recognized that people's behaviour must be understood on the basis of how they interact with the situation and not just on the basis of understanding the person or situation alone.

Use of tests for decision-making

Most of us are primarily interested in using tests to help us make decisions. In making decisions we are essentially making predictions about the future. The employer deciding to hire one applicant rather than another is predicting that the person hired will perform better than the applicants who were not offered jobs. Similarly, a school using a test to identify children for additional mathematics teaching is predicting that selected children will benefit from more appropriate teaching in that setting than if they remained with the other children for normal classroom teaching. In this situation a decision is also being made about how best to allocate teaching resources, with additional resources being concentrated on the children who need extra help in mathematics rather than on the class of children as a whole.

We also all make decisions for ourselves. We have to choose what jobs to apply for, what college courses to attend, and so on. In making these decisions, we recognize that our decisions will have consequences. Is it a good job? Do I need to study this subject if I want to become an architect?

Few decisions are made exclusively on the basis of test results. Typically, other factors influence the judgements that are made, so that the final decision is made on the basis of a combination of different sorts of information, including personal preferences and value judgements. Even official decisions about policies or procedures are affected by these factors. Most decisions are made without recourse to the use of psychological tests but there are many decisions where information from tests can be shown to be relevant, that is, to lead to the choice with the greatest probability of being correct or of leading to the desired outcome.

Sometimes there are other constraints on the decision-making process. There are only a limited number of jobs available, so while an employer may decide not to appoint people if they do not achieve a satisfactory level of performance in the selection process, additional jobs are unlikely to be created if there are more good candidates than vacancies (although this does happen sometimes). Similarly, in educational and clinical settings the resources for treatment may be limited. For example, there may be a fixed number of places on an intervention programme or in a special education group, and these have to be allocated on the basis of greatest need.

Regardless of how decisions are made, there are several factors that have to be borne in mind in the choices that we make. First of all, it is clear that the different alternatives may have different values to us. Sometimes we are genuinely indifferent to the two alternatives and might as well toss a coin to decide between them. In most other cases, it is readily apparent that one outcome is more desirable than another. The employer wants to employ the more productive workers, the job applicant to be offered the best job, the student to go to the best college, and so on. (The definition of 'best' will vary between people. For one person the best job is the most interesting, for another the most well paid, and so on.)

Secondly, we must realize that outcomes from decisions are rarely absolutely predictable. There is nearly always some possibility that the wrong decision will be made. In adopting a rational approach to decision-making we have to balance the probability of achieving our preferred outcome against the value of that outcome to us.

The cost of making the decision is another factor that can affect how the decision is made. Although not typically an issue with the use of psychological tests, in some circumstances, for example in screening programmes where a large number of people have to be tested to identify a very small number of people needing treatment, the cost of screening could outweigh the benefits. Many medical screening programmes are targeted at people in particular age groups because it is only in those age groups where prevalence is highest that screening is seen as a cost effective preventive measure.

Tests are therefore useful in decision-making if they increase the probability of the more valued outcome being achieved, and the additional cost of using the test does not outweigh the benefits. A test will be useful for selecting employees if it increases the proportion of high performers that are employed. The increase in productivity will almost certainly be greater than the cost of testing. By placing people in jobs that they find interesting, labour turnover may also be reduced, and thus costs associated with recruiting and training will be minimized. Similarly, a test will be useful in an educational setting if it means that a child receives more appropriate teaching and the school is able to allocate teaching resources more effectively.

Different types of decisions

The decisions for which tests are used can be classified in several ways. For convenience, the model that is presented here is based on that used by Cronbach (1990). He distinguished four uses of tests:

- Classification

- Evaluation of programmes

- Promoting self-understanding

- Scientific inquiry.

These are described in detail below.

Classification

Classification involves assigning someone to one category rather than another. The implication of the assignment is that an individual will be treated differently as a result.

There are several different types of decision that fall under this heading.

Selection: Here the decision is yes or no, as in the decision to employ or not to employ someone, to promote someone or to offer a college place. Selection decisions involve just two categories – acceptance and rejection.

Screening: This usually describes an initial decision-making process to determine whom to investigate further. Examples are the shortlisting of job applicants to decide whom to invite for the second stage of the selection process, the use of checklists with young children to identify for further assessment those who may be developmentally delayed; the use of sight or hearing tests in schools to identify whom to refer for treatment and so on. These are also usually two-category decisions, but depending on the situation it may be those who 'pass' or those who 'fail' the test who are investigated further.

Certification: Here the decision is whether someone is qualified to a certain standard. For example, the examination to determine whether a doctor is qualified to practise, the driving test, school or college exams. In contrast to selection, where only a small proportion of applicants are usually chosen, any number of candidates could, in theory, be certified provided they reach the required standard.

Placement: In this case the decision leads to everyone being offered some kind of treatment. This is sometimes called **allocation**. For example, when children are streamed into different ability groups for science teaching, the level or amount of instruction is assumed to vary for each of the different groups.

Diagnosis: This implies explanation. It should not mean just giving a label, but also selecting or developing an appropriate treatment plan. This is frequently associated with illness, dysfunction or distress. Considerable expertise is usually required on the part of the person making a diagnosis, who would be expected to have specialist knowledge in both assessment and treatment. Much of the testing and assessment carried out by clinical and educational psychologists falls into this category.

Sometimes one type of classification decision follows another. Applicants for jobs are selected and then placed. People are screened and those selected for further investigation are diagnosed.

It should be noted that the term 'classification' is sometimes used to refer to placement decisions where all the individuals assessed are assigned or allocated to a treatment. This is in contrast to selection decisions where only a subset is chosen or accepted.

Evaluation of programmes

Assessment methods and psychological tests are important aids in evaluating educational interventions and social programmes. It can be argued that an exam tests the adequacy of classroom instruction or the teacher as much as it tests the students. The results may indicate which subject areas should be given more attention in the next academic year, or suggest where teaching methods should be altered. Similarly, if an employer carries out a stress audit, the results can be used to identify jobs that need to be redesigned to make them less stressful as well as to estimate potential take-up for a stress management training programme.

Particular programmes that psychologists have been concerned with include nursery and early childhood intervention programmes, such as Project Headstart in the United States. Initial hopes were that the programme would help prepare children from disadvantaged backgrounds for school. Longer-term follow-up studies have suggested that participants in the programme benefited in a wide variety of ways. Compared with non-participants, they were less likely to drop out of school, less likely to have criminal records, more likely to have jobs, and so on. The social benefits from the programme are as, and possibly more, significant than the educational benefits measured in terms of school performance. The initial evaluation studies did find some short-term educational benefits from the programme but it is only recently that long-term follow-up studies have suggested significant, largely unexpected, benefits from the project.

Not all programmes that are evaluated are successful but, on the other hand, few evaluation studies stop programmes. There are frequently many stakeholders in large projects, with a wide variety of views on what counts as a benefit. Large-scale national or government-sponsored programmes often have their own in-built momentum. In such circumstances the most an evaluator might hope to achieve is a 'course correction', some sort of change of emphasis in the balance of the programme.

Is a training programme for unemployed people successful if it is found that participants are more likely to get jobs than non-participants? The answer may be yes or may be no. Any judgement will probably be affected by views about the quality of the jobs obtained.

Apart from the political nature of many evaluation studies, a distinguishing characteristic of the use of tests in these settings is that test results are used to compare groups and subgroups rather than the performance of individuals. This has important implications for the types of tests that might be used. For example, we would be less concerned about measurement error in a group situation than if we were making predictions about individuals. As a consequence we would consider using shorter and less reliable tests. (This issue is discussed further in Chapter 5.)

Promoting self-understanding

Increasingly, tests are being used in situations where the person who takes the test is the main user of the test results. In part this has come about because of a change in attitudes. Whereas, for example, career counsellors used to give advice on the basis of their interpretation of the test results, now they are much more likely to discuss the test results with their clients and recognize that clients must ultimately make their own decisions about their career plans.

Even in organizational settings there is now frequently much more dialogue between individuals and their managers about the allocation of work roles. Many employers are adapting their assessment centres to offer their employees the opportunity to use the results to plan their future development. In these 'development centres', there may be tensions between whether the individual or the organization owns the information generated by the assessment (see Jackson and Yeates, 1993) but participants will certainly have access to the results of the assessment exercises and tests.

Trainability tests can also promote self-understanding. These tests are based on the idea that observing job applicants carrying out a sample of work behaviour is a good **predictor** of training success. One advantage of the use of trainability tests is that potential applicants may deselect themselves on the basis of their own ratings of their test performance (Downs *et al.*, 1978). In a trainability test, applicants are given a task to complete, followed by a short period of instruction and then asked to repeat the task. Test performance is measured by the degree of improvement between the first and second attempts.

Finally, in educational settings there is also increasing recognition that both students and colleges need to be informed about each other so that they can make appropriate decisions. Students choose courses and colleges just as much as courses and colleges choose students.

Scientific inquiry

In contrast to the other three categories where tests are being used to make practical decisions, the decisions that research psychologists are trying to make are between rival scientific theories and hypotheses. Such studies frequently use standard versions of published tests, but in some circumstances investigators develop their own tests or procedures. Such measures need to be evaluated against the same measurement criteria as published tests. The scale of this activity should not be underestimated. Dawis (1992) notes that in a single year authors publishing articles in the American Psychological Association's *Journal of Counseling Psychology* used 115 newly-constructed or little-used instruments.

These four categories of decisions for which tests are used are not mutually exclusive. A particular use of tests may fit into more than one of these categories. Decisions to do with classification and programme evaluation are usually made for the benefit of institutions or organizations. When decisions are made for promoting self-understanding or classification they are made about individuals, if not always for their benefit. The use of tests for programme evaluation or scientific inquiry is concerned with general knowledge and practical policies.

It is possible to contrast an approach to testing that is empirical, pragmatic and utilitarian with one that puts more emphasis on insight, understanding and theoretical concerns. While for many individuals the attraction of using tests is their ability to generate information that addresses practical concerns, the challenge is to be aware of the range of contextual issues affecting test performance. Only if these are borne in mind can interpretation of test results be made with sufficient insight and understanding.

How useful are tests?

One hundred years ago there were no psychological tests. Now their use is widespread. We need to understand how this came about, and why.

The first successful test, the prototype for all psychological tests, not only intelligence tests, was developed in France by Binet and Simon before the First World War as part of a French Government commission to study procedures for the education of children with learning difficulties. Children's performance on the tests they devised was evaluated by comparing their performance with that of other children of similar age to give what Binet called a child's 'mental level'. Their tests were innovative because of both the type of questions that were used and the scoring procedures they developed. They are the forerunners of most tests of ability designed to be administered on a one-to-one basis.

However, inasmuch as necessity is the mother of invention, the widespread use of tests can largely be put down to the need of the US army, when they entered World War I, to assess the suitability of, and allocate appropriate jobs to, large numbers of recruits. This was the world's first large-scale testing programme using ability tests. While its success in helping the US military has been disputed, it certainly provided a major impetus to the subsequent development and use of tests.

As a result, the 1920s saw the rapid expansion of the testing movement. Group ability tests started to be used in schools while, in clinical settings, psychologists' main role was to conduct the assessment of individual patients with the Stanford-Binet or an equivalent test. In Britain testing in education was promoted by Cyril Burt who had been appointed psychologist to the London County Council in 1913. C. S. Myers also established the National Institute of Industrial Psychology (NIIP) in 1921, which aimed to promote the use of psychological techniques, such as testing, by employers. The first personality measures and interest inventories were also developed at this time.

Some US commentators (e.g. Anastasi, 1982) have suggested that much of this testing was indiscriminate and 'may have done as much to retard as to advance the progress of psychological testing' (p12). However, she suggests that several important lessons were learnt about the limitations of these early tests. One example is their focus on only certain aspects of intelligence, frequently verbal and to a lesser extent numerical and **spatial** abilities. Psychologists also noted that an individual's performance often varied between different parts of the same test.

One of the most important series of experiments using psychological tests was organized in Britain by the NIIP in the late 1930s. These were concerned with evaluating the impact of the use of ability tests in vocational guidance. The findings demonstrated the superiority of vocational guidance incorporating ability test results over guidance given without such tests.

In Britain, psychological tests have had their greatest impact during and since World War II. For many years entry to secondary schools at age eleven was determined by test performance. The 'eleven-plus' was controversial. Assumptions were made about intellectual development and the three-quarters of all children who failed (with some variation in the proportion passing in different parts of the country, influenced largely by the number of grammar school places available), were allocated to a markedly inferior education in contrast to the high quality academic education offered to those who passed. Performance in the test was influenced by the quality of schooling received in the primary years. It is also interesting to note that in some localities where more girls were found to obtain high scores on the eleven-plus than boys, separate cut-off scores were used so that the same percentage of boys and girls were deemed to have passed the exam. Legal and ethical issues in fixing appropriate cut-off scores when selecting people will be discussed in Chapter 6 'How to judge tests'.

The main argument for using tests in large-scale selection programmes, such as the eleven-plus, has been that by using tests the selection process is more systematic and objective. On these grounds alone it can be argued that testing has promoted fairness despite some of the obvious shortcomings of testing. It might even be argued that the impact of the testing programme was one of the reasons that the educational assumptions underlying the decision to stream children at this age were challenged. However, many working-class children benefited from the eleven-plus because they would have been excluded from receiving an academic education if more subjective selection processes had been used. Similarly, there is considerable evidence that the use of tests in large-scale military placement programmes during World War II had positive outcomes, such as fewer people failing or being asked to repeat their training. Testing has, therefore, been demonstrated to offer significant benefits both for individuals who, by passing tests, have gained opportunities that would otherwise have been denied to them, and to organizations that have reduced training costs and employed more productive workers.

Of course, this does not mean that all testing programmes will have positive outcomes. The challenge is to use tests appropriately and be aware both of their strengths and of their limitations.

The need to evaluate tests

As the number of tests has multiplied, the problem of choosing between tests has become ever more challenging. Hoping to put the bad tests out of business, the American psychologist, Buros, started to publish the *Mental Measurements Yearbooks*. The first few merely provided bibliographies on tests, but from 1938 the yearbook took on its present form and began including critical reviews of tests by experts plus a complete list of references for a particular test. Never an annual publication, the *Twelfth Mental Measurements Yearbook* was published in 1995. Although the extent to which Buros achieved his original goal is debatable, the yearbook and its companion publications provide an invaluable source of independent information about tests. The *Mental Measurements Yearbooks* are now published by the University of Nebraska (see Chapter 8 and the sources of further information for more detailed information about the *Mental Measurements Yearbooks*).

As Cronbach (1970) has noted, one personality test first published in 1935 was still a best seller after repeated critical comments. Influencing test users' behaviour is, perhaps, not straightforward after all. This point underscores the issue that provision of information alone does not necessarily improve practice. Modern approaches to improving standards of testing emphasize the responsibility of the test user for ensuring that tests are used appropriately.

We have already noted how testing continues to evolve. Although underlying ideas change relatively slowly, the rate of production of new tests and the frequency with which old tests are revised continue to increase. This has meant that getting up-to-date information on particular tests becomes more and more difficult for the user. In Britain this has led the BPS to commission reviews of commonly used tests (Bartram *et al.*, 1990, 1992 and Bartram *et al.*, 1995) and also the development of open learning material on psychological testing (Bartram and Lindley, 1994). These developments are discussed in greater detail in Chapter 8 'How to find out about tests' and Chapter 9 'Becoming a test user'. It is interesting to note, however, that many tests first published up to fifty years ago are still being used, although they will have been revised and updated in the meantime.

One of the difficulties is that once a test has been developed, published and has developed a user base, there is considerable investment on the part of users and publishers to stay with the same test. Sometimes, even when revised versions of existing tests are produced, there are test users who wish to continue using the previous version of the test. This means that it sometimes takes several years for a new version of an existing test to replace the previous version.

Summary

This chapter has discussed why we use tests. It has done this by identifying that the key purpose for carrying out any assessment process is to make decisions. We need to make decisions because all people are different. Psychologists have developed psychological tests as the practical technology for assessing individual differences. Subsequent chapters of this book will elaborate the underlying measurement principles that make possible the use of psychological tests.

This chapter has also set out in a general way the types of decisions for which tests can be used and has raised some of the issues that have to be considered in the 'real world' application of tests. It also notes how large-scale testing programmes developed and how this led to an increase in test use. This, in turn, raised the need for more information on how to evaluate tests.

3 What is a psychological test?

If asked to define what a 'test' is, most of us would probably think of tests taken in school or a driving test. On the face of it, these are quite different experiences. The school test usually consists of a set of questions to which written answers must be given. It may involve choosing between alternative answers – a multiple-choice test. The driving test involves demonstrating that one is able to drive a car safely. It now includes a written test but the primary component of the test is driving a car: the driving examiner observes the candidate's driving performance and makes a decision on whether that performance can be judged to be safe enough for the individual to be allowed to drive on the roads unsupervised.

What are the similarities between these two types of test? First of all, both tests involve sampling the activity. For practical reasons, for example the time available, the tests cannot cover all the knowledge and skills required. For the school test to be fair, questions must be chosen to be representative of what the teacher has been teaching. In the driving test, while certain specific manoeuvres can be required of all candidates, the ability to handle some situations will only be observed if certain conditions are encountered – for example, dealing with heavy traffic or driving in the rain.

Secondly, the procedures aim to be standardized and **systematic**, that is the same for all people taking the test. In the school test this is achieved by asking the same questions of all candidates. In the driving test this can only be partially achieved by requiring people to perform the same manoeuvres because, as noted above, other factors that may affect performance cannot be standardized. However, the driving test can be carried out in a systematic manner.

For a test to meet the requirement of being standardized and systematic, the assessment of the quality of performance must also be carried out in the same way for all candidates. This means that the marking or scoring of the test must also be done in a standardized and systematic manner.

There should be clear rules for defining what counts as a correct answer or satisfactory performance.

In many tests, what counts as a correct answer is clear cut, there is only one possible correct answer and other answers are clearly incorrect. For example, if asked to identify the next number in the series: 2, 4, 8, 16, ..., there is only one correct answer: 32. In other situations the acceptability of a particular answer or performance is a matter of judgement. For example, in the driving test the examiner must make a judgement about the competence of the person being examined in relation to reversing around a corner based on factors such as the care they take in ensuring it is safe to perform the manoeuvre, their skill at controlling their speed, their ability to judge distance between the kerb and the car, and so on.

In other cases a judgement must be made about the *degree* of correctness. For example, an ability test might ask a child what they would do if they found some money lying in the street. The test administrator has to record the child's answer and then follow a standard procedure in scoring it. To meet our criteria of being a test, these judgements must be made in the same way for all candidates. If not, there is inconsistency in the scoring procedure. In this case the test manual, which describes how the test should be used, would contain detailed instructions outlining how different replies should be scored, so that the reply 'I would keep the money' might get a score of zero, a reply 'I would take it home and ask my parents what to do' a score of one, and an answer 'I would hand it in at a police station' a score of two. Clearly there are many other answers a child might give to this question and so the test manual has to outline how a range of typical answers might be scored, and give guidance as to the underlying principles that have been used in scoring answers so that the examiner can score other replies in a consistent way. This implies that, as part of the development process for the test, the question has been asked of many children so that consistent rules for scoring could be developed.

In other tests, such as personality tests or interest inventories, there are no right or wrong answers and the decision is not whether an answer given is correct but whether it can be allocated consistently to a particular response category. For example, the question, 'On a Saturday evening would you rather: (a) stay at home and read a book, (b) unsure, (c) go out to a party?' might be one of a series of questions intended to decide how outgoing a person is. There is no right answer to this question. Answer (c) might score two on being outgoing, answer (b) one and answer (a) zero. When replies to a series of similar questions are added up, an individual can be given a score which can be compared with that of other people to determine that person's relative degree of 'outgoingness'. Of course, a great deal of effort goes into choosing the content for such a test, writing questions, trying them out, rejecting some and modifying others, seeing whether individuals' replies are consistent from day to day, whether their scores predict how they will behave, or match up with **peer ratings** from their friends, and so on.

Describing the process of test development is beyond the scope of this book. Key measurement issues that users of tests need to be concerned about when they are using test scores are discussed in Chapters 5 and 6 but two key terms – **reliability** and **validity** – need highlighting. Reliability refers to the accuracy of measurement and validity is about the extent to which a test measures what it is expected to.

Definitions

Two examples of definitions of a psychological test from leading US psychologists are:

> *A test is a systematic procedure for observing behavior and describing it with the aid of numerical scales or fixed categories* (Cronbach).

> *A psychological test is essentially an objective and standardized measure of a sample of behaviour* (Anastasi).

Both these definitions cover the points noted above that tests can only **sample** psychological characteristics and that measurement is based on standardized and systematic procedures as far as possible. This implies that the testing procedures, apparatus and scoring have been fixed so that they are, as far as possible, precisely the same at different times and places and regardless of who administers them.

Tests also vary in the extent to which they are objective. An objective procedure is one where every observer would produce an identical account of what took place. In practice, **objectivity** is a matter of degree that can be judged by the extent to which independent observers agree in the scores they assign. The less agreement there is, the more subjective is the scoring procedure. Scoring a multiple-choice maths test is completely objective, while scoring English essays or evaluating an individual's behaviour in a group discussion, even when both have clear scoring rules, will be less objective. Measuring the degree of consistency between different observers or markers is one way of evaluating consistency and degree of objectivity. If scorers possess relevant expert knowledge, have been trained and given clear scoring rules, consistency between different observers will almost certainly be improved and the subjectivity of scoring will be lessened.

Objectivity and **standardization** are closely linked. Multiple-choice tests that have correct answers, or where each reply option is assigned to a response category, have objective scoring procedures, although the meaning of the particular score an individual obtains will require interpretation. However, a test with variable procedures, such as a driving test, may be scored using definite rules while, alternatively, a test with standardized procedures may have judgmental scoring – for example, where spoken replies have to be scored by the person administering the test.

Psychological tests have been developed as measurement procedures and, as with most measurement, this means producing results that are quantifiable. Test scores, therefore, are typically given as numbers, which facilitates their analysis by mathematical and statistical means. This is not always the case, however, and sometimes individuals are just being allocated to a category or group. One example of this would be those who have passed their driving test.

It is important to note the broad scope of these definitions. They cover not only paper-and-pencil tests but also observational techniques, tests involving the manipulation of apparatus and so on. Certain sorts of interview would also qualify as tests under these definitions, as would assessment centre exercises such as group discussions, role plays, or in-tray exercises.

Standardization as an ideal concept

In practice, standardization is only an ideal concept. There are many factors that can affect an individual's performance on a test and that cannot be standardized between candidates. One factor that is very difficult to control is a person's state of mind – whether someone slept well the night before or whether they have just had a row with their boss. Another factor will be the purpose for which the test is being taken. Taking a test as part of a selection process for a job is very different from taking a test as part of a career counselling process. Unfortunately, it is not straightforward to predict how personal circumstances or the purpose of the testing will affect the performance of a particular individual. For some people, knowing that a job offer might depend on their test performance will act as spur for them to produce their best performance, while others will find that the extra stress hinders their performance.

The degree of **rapport** established between the test taker and the person administering the test can also affect test performance. In some settings, especially in clinical and educational assessment, psychologists have to be quite flexible in their approach to testing. For example when testing young children, it may be necessary to present the test as part of a game to get their co-operation to participate.

As well as individual circumstances affecting test performance, there are cultural factors that can also affect how individuals respond to tests. Race, gender and social class are all examples of cultural factors that may affect test performance (see Chapter 6).

The fact that standardization can never be achieved should not lead us to despair of the benefits of using tests. However, it is yet another reminder of the importance of context to any real-life testing and of the inherent limitations of any measurement procedure.

Types of test

Tests can be grouped in a variety of ways. For example, whether they can be administered to individuals on a one-to-one basis, to a group in a classroom situation, or both; whether they are paper-and-pencil tests or involve the manipulation of apparatus; whether the tests are timed or not; whether responses to the questions are open-ended or forced-choice, and so on. All these sorts of information about particular tests may be relevant in some circumstances.

For many purposes it is convenient to distinguish two broad categories of tests. Cronbach (1990) calls them tests of **maximum performance** and measures of **typical response**. Essentially, this is a distinction between those tests where there are correct answers to questions and those where the reply is indicative of how the person might respond in a given situation. Figure 3.1 lists the headings that are commonly used to describe tests.

Tests of maximum performance

These are tests where the person taking the test is asked to perform to the best of their ability. There are right answers and wrong answers. They are frequently referred to as tests of ability, and can be broken down into the following two broad categories:

Tests of general mental ability cover tests measuring abilities important for thinking. They are often called 'intelligence' tests but intelligence is a word full of surplus meaning, and test interpretation is more straightforward if the term 'intelligence' is not used.

It is useful to distinguish between tests of general mental ability that can be administered to groups and those tests designed for individual

---

Figure 3.1 Types of Psychological Test

1. Tests of Maximum Performance
   Measures of General Mental Ability
      (i) Individual Tests
      (ii) Group Tests

   Measures of Special Abilities

2. Tests of Typical Response
   Observation
      (i) Standardized Observation Procedures
      (ii) Field Observation in Natural Settings

   Self-Report
      (i) Interest Inventories
      (ii) Personality Measures
      (iii) Inferential Methods

---

assessment. Tests designed for individual assessment on a one-to-one basis may require the examiner to time responses, use apparatus, or write down replies to questions. Such tests are mainly used by clinical and educational psychologists and require considerable expertise if they are to be used properly. Group tests are usually paper-and-pencil tests but these are now sometimes equivalent computer-administered versions. They nearly always have a forced-choice answer format where an individual has to select the right answer from a set of alternatives. The guide for test takers (page 147) includes sample questions from such tests.

Tests of special abilities cover tests designed to measure special skills (e.g. musical ability), knowledge or competence in a particular area (e.g. a driving test, a reading test), or special aptitude (e.g. clerical aptitude). These tests are distinguished from general mental ability tests by their content and by their usefulness in predicting performance in a specific area.

These tests include those designed to measure **achievement** or proficiency which are sometimes contrasted with aptitude tests that are intended to predict success. Cronbach notes the somewhat artificial nature of this distinction, as performance on *any* test reflects development and learning (achievement) and can be used for prediction (aptitude). It has been suggested that the distinction reflects underlying views on the causes of individual differences in abilities. Are they regarded as fixed and to be used for matching people to activities, or as measures of past experience that can be topped up by training?

Measures of typical response

These are tests designed to measure typical behaviour where there are no right or wrong answers. Two approaches characterize measurement in this area:

Observation can be conducted in a standardized setting or in natural surroundings. In both types of setting it is assumed that trained observers record aspects of an individual's performance for assessment by watching the behaviour directly or in video recordings. Observation is frequently used by clinical and educational psychologists.

Sometimes observation takes place in contrived situations to study responses that would otherwise occur only occasionally, or to watch people brought together specially in a particular situation. Some exercises at assessment centres fall under this heading. Observation in these circumstances is sometimes referred to as a **performance** or situational test and in such circumstances the purpose of testing is frequently disguised.

Observations can be carried out in natural surroundings, for example in the classroom or the workplace. To examine the degree of co-operation between children, educational psychologists might observe a video recording of children at a pre-school play group.

What is important about observational techniques is the extent to which they are carried out in a systematic manner. The extent to which ratings of work performance are based on observations that could be considered systematic, and the extent to which scoring is consistent is an example. Would different observers classify behaviour in the same way? Developing appropriate scoring procedures, so that what is observed can be categorized in the same way, and training observers to achieve consistency in scoring are, therefore, an important part of any assessment process based on observation.

Being able to record on videotape is obviously a tremendous advantage as the observer does not have to be physically present, and colleagues can also be involved in judging and evaluating what has been recorded. In addition, video recordings provide the observer with a permanent record that can be viewed more than once, and kept to allow comparisons to be made before and after treatment. They are also particularly useful for developing scoring procedures and training observers.

Ethical issues are important if observation is taking place without the subject's knowledge, or if the purpose is disguised. In such situations invasion of privacy can be countered by obtaining informed consent. This should include the opportunity for the removal of material from records if behaviour has been observed which the person being observed wishes to remain confidential.

Observation-based procedures are not widely used because of their great expense, although the use of assessment centres, which usually include observation as well as tests and interviews, is popular with employers for selecting managers. On its own, observation is of most interest to clinical and educational psychologists and also for research applications in psychology and related social science disciplines.

Self-report is used by psychologists as their main source of information about people's preferences, interests and habits. Questionnaires, sometimes called 'measures' rather than tests because there are no right or wrong answers, are used to ask people to describe their preferences for different activities or how they might behave in a given situation. This approach is based on the assumption that individuals know their own preferences, interests and so on, and are, therefore, the best possible source of information about themselves. However, psychologists recognize that people are not necessarily consistent from one situation to the next, and what happened in the past is only an imperfect guide to the future.

People's ability to be impartial observers of themselves may also vary. Psychologists who design and construct such tests are often concerned about potential distortion of the test results or '**faking**' by the person taking the test. There is a considerable literature on how to deal with what are technically called '**response sets**', such as the tendency to use what are thought to be the more socially desirable response categories or give what might be perceived as the 'right' answer in a particular situation. For example, if you were applying for a job as a salesperson, wouldn't you be more likely to say 'always', rather than 'sometimes' or 'never' in reply to the question: 'Do you enjoy meeting new people?'

Measures are usually categorized by content area, the main two being:

- *Interest inventories* designed to measure occupational interests and preferences, mainly used for career counselling.
- *Personality measures* designed either to measure specific personality dimensions or a broad set of such dimensions that characterize behaviour.

A third group of self-report measures is based on a particular approach to assessment:

- *Inferential methods* include testing procedures where the way a person performs, that is the process of answering or the approach taken, is being assessed. They also include **projective techniques** where the person is presented with an unstructured task or situation and has to create a response for interpretation. These methods include sentence completion tasks and tests involving interpreting pictures or inkblots. A test **item** might show a picture of a child playing with a toy and another child saying, 'It's my turn now', and the test taker has to invent a reply or series of possible replies that the first child might have given.

Most tests in the interest **inventory** and personality measures categories are paper-and-pencil tests designed for group administration, although in some settings, for example in counselling, they may be individually administered. Interest inventories and personality measures are widely used in non-clinical applications and issues concerning their use are discussed in subsequent chapters. The class of measures labelled 'inferential methods' is mainly of interest for in-depth assessment on a one-to-one basis in clinical settings where the test user must be highly trained. A key issue in their use is the extent to which they can be scored in a systematic manner, that is whether different people would make the same interpretation of a subject's responses. They will not be discussed further as their use is not widespread outside clinical settings.

Limitations

Any classification procedure is likely to have its limitations. Tests originally designed for one purpose have been found to be useful for another. Style of performance on an ability test could be used to infer information about personality, for example, the ability to plan ahead.

Cronbach (1990) also counsels that 'maximum performance is a convenient fiction' (p37). It reflects the approach to be taken to the test but, just as in physical activities, most of us could improve our test performances with training or practice. This has important implications for the concept of fairness in testing. The role of practice and coaching in relation to test performance will be discussed further in Chapter 7.

Similarly, it is debatable whether there are really no right or wrong answers when measures of typical behaviour are used for purposes such as selecting people for jobs. Furthermore, it is difficult to believe that, in some circumstances, the context in which the test is being taken will not

influence an individual's choice of response category. The broader implications of these issues will be discussed in Chapter 4 'Where tests are
used'.

Recent technical developments

Psychologists have for many years anticipated the effect computers would
have on psychological testing. However, it is only since the late 1980s that
the new technology has had a major impact on practice, although the use
of computers in psychological testing and assessment dates back to the
1960s.

The American Psychological Association published its latest *Guidelines
for Computer-based Tests and Interpretations* in 1986 out of a concern that new
computer-based approaches to testing should meet the same ethical, professional and technical standards that apply to traditional forms of testing.

The rapid increase in the availability and use of computers in testing is
most obvious in the following areas:

- test administration
- item banks
- adaptive testing
- scoring and test interpretation
- displays.

Test administration: The computer has numerous advantages as a test
administrator. It can administer tests in a more standardized way and also
tailor an ability test to the individual by asking an easier question if someone gets an answer wrong, or a more difficult question if they get an
answer right. In some applications this allows more precise measurement
than could be achieved by conventional testing. (See the section on adaptive testing, page 36.)

Other advantages include the computer's immunity from boredom,
fatigue or lapses of attention. If suitably programmed, the computer will
not mind if the person taking the test does not respond for hours or,
alternatively, it can be programmed to send a signal, perhaps an audible
tone, after a set period to act as a reminder to respond.

The computer is also able to record additional information about the
test performance, such as time taken to respond to each test item, something that could not easily be done for traditional paper-and-pencil versions of tests, and that would be impossible in group sessions. Another

major advantage is that the computer can usually score the test and produce a report of the results instantly.

However, a computer cannot observe whether someone is distressed and it cannot answer a test taker's questions. The testing session as a whole still needs to be supervised so that a record is available of any special circumstances applying in a particular session.

It should always be remembered that a computerized version of a test is not the same as the paper-and-pencil version, and scores on forms of a test that have been administered in different ways should not be compared directly. It cannot be assumed that either the difficulty of items or the reliability of the whole test will remain unchanged when a test is presented by computer, even if the same test items are used.

For example, test performance can be affected by familiarity with the use of a keyboard. This is one reason why some tests use specially designed key pads or other input devices. Procedures also need to be in place to allow test takers to correct mistakes or change their answers. Some tests ask respondents to confirm their answers. In this way test takers are given the opportunity to change their answers. Other activities which are quite straightforward on a paper-and-pencil version of a test, such as going back to look over your answers, are no longer so easy to manage on a computerized version of the same test.

If a test is designed to be timed, the timing may need to be changed for the computer-based version. On the other hand, computerizing a test may remove the need for timing, which is often required as much for administrative convenience as anything else.

Particular issues affect different sorts of tests. On computer administered ability tests, respondents will not usually have the option to skip items and/or to go back to a question. Normally each question has to be attempted.

Item banks: For the traditional paper-and-pencil test there may be only one or two versions of the test available. Sometimes these versions are designed to be equivalent forms of the same test. At other times the versions differ, perhaps being designed for different age groups, so that a version for children would contain easier items than the version of the same test for adults.

All the questions in the different versions of a particular test can be considered to be the **item bank** for the test. Increasingly, test developers are constructing large banks of items classified by content and difficulty level which are stored on computer. These can be used to generate a large number of different test versions almost on demand. This can prove particularly valuable for large-scale testing programmes, for example in educational settings, where a similar version of the same test is required every year but where there might be fears about the confidentiality of the test items. In the past, if a candidate has taken the test before, there was also a strong possibility that the second test performance would be improved because the test taker would remember the answers given to some of the questions from the previous time.

Such item banks are also required for adaptive testing. However, it should be noted that often there are practical difficulties in constructing large banks of equivalent items.

Adaptive testing: One attraction of computer-based testing is the potential opportunity to tailor the questions to a particular test taker. In a conventional ability test, for example, items are frequently presented in order of increasing difficulty. Some people will find the first few items trivial to solve, being really stretched only on the later, more difficult items. At the other extreme, some people will be disheartened by their inability to answer even the early items. A computer, because it can score each answer straight away, can rapidly move to testing people at the limit of their performance. This should allow more accurate assessment and could also save time as test takers do not have to waste time completing easy test items or attempting very difficult items.

In practice, calibrating items in terms of level of difficulty is not a simple process. Remember that candidates who have taken the test need to be given scores that reflect their performance relative to each other even though they have not answered the same set of questions. Data need to be collected from a large number of people to assess item difficulty accurately and inevitably some people find one type of item more difficult than another, so analysis has to focus on a particular type of item. This might mean, for example, writing a set of items that involve identifying the next number in a series and then measuring the difficulty of each of the items.

It is for this reason that computerized versions of tests are frequently broken down into sub-tests with similar item content, whereas paper-and-pencil versions frequently present a series of items with a variety of styles within a single test (e.g. a mix of verbal and diagrammatic items).

Scoring and test interpretation: Computers have been used to score tests for many years. However, when tests are also administered on computer they can be scored immediately. Potentially, test takers can be given immediate feedback on whether they have answered items correctly or not.

In addition to calculating numerical scores, computers have also been programmed to generate individual test interpretations by comparing an individual's performance on the test with the performance of other people. The use of such interpretations is particularly widespread with personality measures, and to a lesser extent with interest inventories. In these situations, where a single test often generates scores on a large number of **scales**, much of the skill of interpretation is based not just on the meaning given to individual scores but on the interaction between scores. In these circumstances it is the **profile** of scores that is being interpreted and not just the individual scale scores. For example, with an interest inventory it might be the individual's order of preference for the interest categories that is used to suggest possible occupations. Similarly, with a personality measure it is the combinations of high and low scores on different scales that is used to generate a report. Figure 3.2 shows an example of the profile sheet that is used to present an individual's scores from the Sixteen Personality Factor Questionnaire (16PF).

The American Psychological Association *Guidelines for Computer-based Tests and Interpretations* (1986) stress that 'interpretative reports should only be used in conjunction with professional judgement'. This is important because otherwise vital contextual information about individual test takers or the situations under which they were tested is likely to be ignored. Regardless of how a test interpretation is produced, a qualified professional must take responsibility for it.

The current state of computer-based test interpretation is such that the sophistication of available interpretations varies considerably. Some do little more than report scores and compare them with the scores achieved by other groups of people. Others offer narrative reports that might appear similar to reports written by an expert. Computer programs are now also available to help the test user to write their own interpretation or to customize a standard report.

The use of computers to generate narrative reports is controversial. Some have not been validated and they may offer little more than one person's judgement. A particular danger is that they appear plausible and authoritative because of the way they are presented. There is evidence from a number of research studies that when presented with reports made up of general, stereotyped statements, most people accept them (Forer, 1949; Stagner, 1958). Meehl as long ago as 1956 suggested that this should be called the '**Barnum effect**' after Phineas T Barnum, the American showman, who is credited with the famous quotes: 'There's a sucker born every minute' and 'You can fool most of the people most of the time.'

In one study (Stagner, 1958), 68 personnel managers who had completed a personality questionnaire were each presented with the same fake

Figure 3.2 Sixteen Personality Factor Questionnaire (16PF5) Profile Sheet

SIXTEEN PERSONALITY FACTOR QUESTIONNAIRE FIFTH EDITION (16PF5)

PROFILE SHEET

SURNAME————————————— FORENAME ——————————————

SEX ——————— AGE ——————— DATE——————— NORM GROUP ———————

Instructions:
Write the raw score for each factor in the second column and the sten score in the third column. Starting with Factor A, place a mark over the spot representing the appropriate sten score. Repeat for each factor. Connect the score with straight lines.

PRIMARY FACTORS

Factor	Raw	Sten	Left Meaning	Standard Ten Score (STEN) ← Average → 1 2 3 4 5 6 7 8 9 10	Right Meaning
A: Warmth			More Emotionally Distant from People		Attentive and Warm to Others
B: Reasoning			Fewer Reasoning Items Correct		More Reasoning Items Correct
C: Emotional Stability			Reactive, Emotionally Changeable		Emotionally Stable, Adaptive
E: Dominance			Deferential, Cooperative, Avoids Conflict		Dominant, Forceful
F: Liveliness			Serious, Cautious, Careful		Lively, Animated, Spontaneous
G: Rule-Consciousness			Expedient, Non-conforming		Rule-Conscious, Dutiful
H: Social Boldness			Shy, Threat-Sensitive, Timid		Socially Bold, Venturesome, Thick-Skinned
I: Sensitivity			Objective, Unsentimental		Subjective, Sentimental
L: Vigilance			Trusting, Unsuspecting, Accepting		Vigilant, Suspicious, Sceptical, Wary
M: Abstractedness			Grounded, Practical, Solution-Oriented		Abstracted, Theoretical, Idea-Oriented
N: Privateness			Forthright, Straightforward		Private, Discreet, Non-Disclosing
O: Apprehension			Self-Assured, Unworried		Apprehensive, Self-Doubting, Worried
Q^1: Openness to Change			Traditional, Values the Familiar		Open to Change, Experimenting
Q^2: Self-Reliance			Group-Oriented, Affiliative		Self-Reliant, Individualistic
Q^3: Perfectionism			Tolerates Disorder, Unexacting, Flexible		Perfectionistic, Organized, Self-Disciplined
Q^4: Tension			Relaxed, Placid, Patient		Tense, High Energy, Impatient, Driven

GLOBAL FACTORS

Factor	Raw	Sten	Left Meaning	← Average → 1 2 3 4 5 6 7 8 9 10	Right Meaning
EX: Extraversion			Introverted, Socially Inhibited		Extraverted, Socially Participating
AX: Anxiety			Low Anxiety, Unperturbed		High Anxiety, Perturbable
TM: Tough-Mindedness			Receptive, Open-minded		Tough-Minded, Resolute
IN: Independent			Accommodating, Agreeable, Selfless		Independent, Persuasive, Wilful
SC: Self-Control			Unrestrained, Follows Urges		Self-Controlled, Inhibits Urges

Translated and adapted by permission. 16PF5 copyright © The Institute of Personality and Ability Testing, Inc., 1993. International copyright in all countries under the Berne Union, Buenos Aires, Bilateral, and Universal Copyright Conventions. All property rights reserved by the Institute for Personality and Ability Testing, Inc., 1801 Woodfield Drive, Savoy, Illinois 61874, USA. All rights reserved. Published by The NFER-NELSON Publishing Company Ltd., Darville House, 2 Oxford Road East, Windsor, Berkshire SL4 1DF, UK.   Code 1203 25 4 1(1.94) personality report made up of thirteen statements such as:

- You have a great need for other people to like and admire you.

- You have a tendency to be critical of yourself.

- You pride yourself as an independent thinker and do not accept others' statements without satisfactory proof.

Each personnel manager was then asked to 'validate' the profile by ranking each statement on the five-point scale: Amazingly accurate; Rather good; About half and half; More wrong than right; Almost entirely wrong. Subjects were also asked to give an overall rating to the personality description. Fifty per cent gave an overall evaluation of the personality description as 'amazingly accurate', 40 per cent as 'rather good' and 10 per cent as 'about half and half.' Similar results were also obtained from a group of industrial supervisors.

What are the implications of findings like these for users of personality tests? There are both ethical and technical issues involved. The first is that the provision of valid test interpretations is not a trivial task but requires considerable professional skill and expertise. Anyone who pretends otherwise is misleading potential users. Potential users of computer-generated narrative reports need to be aware of the possible pitfalls in their use and the difficulty in evaluating them. Sometimes the test user will be presented with a choice of different sorts of report for the same test. Reports may vary in level of detail or be designed for different purposes. Not surprisingly, this is an area of current controversy and debate amongst psychologists and experts in personality assessment. *Caveat emptor* – let the buyer beware – seems to be the maxim that purchasers of such systems should hold uppermost in their thoughts.

Figure 3.3 shows excerpts from an interpretative report for the California Psychological Inventory (CPI). Responsible publishers have guidelines on the use of computer-generated narrative reports (see Figure 3.4).

Displays: Computers also allow a variety of new display formats. These can include photographs, moving images, coloured diagrams, and so on. In some situations it is possible to allow candidates to search through databases or work interactively, for example deciding what further information they require to complete a task.

This is an area where there is much current research and it is to be expected that many new specialist applications will become available in the next few years. It is likely that computer-based exercises will increasingly be used in assessment centres.

Figure 3.3 Excerpt from a computer-based CPI Configural Analysis Report

WARNING

CPI — Configural Analysis Report

The reader of this report should be knowledgeable about the CPI and its background. Additionally, it is imperative not to evaluate this report in isolation from other data such as the candidate's recent work performance, biography and achievements. Factors that may influence how this report is interpreted include age, education, cognitive abilities, mental status, occupational listing and reasons for taking the CPI.

PART 1

Hypotheses based on individual scales:

Note: Sections produced in italics are based on the interpretation of the writer of the report. There may be other interpretations. Sections which are not in italics are based on validation in a systematic empirical study.

Dominance (74T)

He is likely to be competitive, controlling and domineering, frequently seeking out power and leadership positions in an aggressive manner. He feels he has to win and may believe he is the only one who can do things right. He is quick to express and defend his opinions. He may be able to follow others effectively, but is still likely to appear assertive. He is sometimes inflexibly dominant, unable to allow others to take the lead.

Social Presence (55-70T)

He generally has high energy and activity levels and will demonstrate a sense of urgency and enthusiasm. He presents himself well in social settings, projecting an air of confidence and poise. He is usually a good talker and not easily embarrassed by having to talk in public or by talking to strangers.

PART 2

Hypotheses from configuration of scales:

High Dominance (74T) and low Good Impression (38T)

He makes little or no effort to ingratiate himself with others: he can be a demanding, domineering, task-oriented autocrat. He wants his own way or else. He feels no urge to protect others, will not behave in a conciliatory way and is not easily influenced by others. He is blunt, direct, uncompromising and argumentative[1].

[1] See Heilbron et al. (1962). Journal of Applied Psychology, 46, 409-416.

Figure 3.4 Oxford Psychologists Press (OPP[1]) Policy on the Publication and Use of Computer-Based Test Interpretations (CBTIs)

General

OPP recognises that CBTI systems have moderate validity and should not be sold to customers on the basis that they have greater accuracy than reports produced by other methods.

Basis of interpretation

Where possible, OPP's computer-based reports will be transparent to the informed user, i.e the link between the scale score and the test will be clear and unambiguous.

OPP will make it plain to customers that the basis of its computer-based interpretations is mainly clinical. That is, the text will have been written by an expert user or users and will embody, therefore, their particular interpretations of the scales.

Where OPP computer reports are wholly or partially based on a systematic, empirical validation procedure (actuarial basis), statements based on data from such a procedure will be clearly indicated (e.g. by using a different typeface).

Use of the reports

OPP CBTI reports are not intended under any circumstances to stand on their own. They are intended to be supplemented by other information such as that collected on a biographical application form or in an interview.

It is not OPP's policy to create reports which give direct guidance or direction (e.g. 'Do not employ this person in Sales'), or even to imply this indirectly. OPP's reports are intended to suggest hypotheses or raise questions.

Availability of the reports

OPP CBTI reports will be made available only to qualified test users accepted by OPP as fully trained and qualified to purchase and interpret the relevant test or tests on which the report is based. OPP does not recognise a category of partially trained users, i.e. qualified to use computer interpretations only.

Third party arrangements

OPP reports are not intended to be shown to third parties (other than the candidate). However, they should never be handed 'blind' to candidates, but always accompanied by oral feedback and opportunities for questioning and discussion.

Parts of OPP CBTI reports may, however, be incorporated in a report to a third party. Any such report should be context related and reflect the test user's own judgements about the degree of relevance of test scores and other information to the purpose of testing.

[1] OPP is a registered trademark of Oxford Psychologists Press.

Figure 3.5 Example of a dynamic computer display

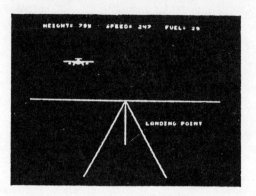

Initial 'Landing' screen display showing digital read outs, horizon and 'runway' with centre-line
Source: Bartram, 1987.

Computers permit very sophisticated simulation and they also have considerable potential for use in training. Many computer-based training programmes can be considered to be tests because they monitor the trainees' progress and provide feedback on performance. It is important to realize that the same rules apply to these procedures as to the development of all other tests. Figure 3.5 presents an example of a display from a test battery designed to assess aptitude for pilot training (Bartram, 1987). It is designed superficially to resemble an aircraft landing simulator. The aircraft symbol is controlled by a joystick and a sliding power controller but the operation and dynamics of the control arrangements have been designed to minimize any positive (or negative) transfer from previous flying experience.

While some tests may look increasingly like sophisticated computer games, it is important to recognize that they differ from computer games because of the way their scoring procedures have been developed and evaluated so that the results of the test can be used in decision-making.

Summary

This chapter has aimed to explain the key features that make up a psychological test and briefly describe some of the main types of test in common use. It is important to realize that, like all other technologies, testing is constantly evolving. These changes are taking place in a variety of ways, not only through the impact of computing on testing practice but also as old ideas are challenged and new ones are introduced.

Key points to note are that:

- tests can only sample behaviour

- standardization is an ideal concept that can only be approximated to in reality

- objectivity in measurement is also a matter of degree but in some circumstances the degree of objectivity, for example of a scoring procedure, can be assessed

- there are two main types of psychological test – tests of maximum performance and tests of typical response

- computers are having a considerable impact on testing practice

- the test user continues to have a professional responsibility to ensure that proper testing procedures are used when computers administer, score or assist in the interpretation of test results.

4 Where tests are used

Would using tests help me?

People in many different situations – personnel managers responsible for recruitment, individuals trying to make career decisions, managers trying to improve team working, or schools wishing to know if children's school performance matches their cognitive ability – need an answer to the question: 'Would using tests help me?' One way to answer this question is to find out how other people use tests and why they find them useful. This should provide some insight into the range of situations in which tests are currently being used and are found to be helpful.

The main reason for using psychological tests is that we believe the results will help us make a decision. This means that we think the information obtained from the test scores will assist us in making some sort of prediction, for example to whom to offer a job, which college course to choose or, if we are using a test for screening, which people to assess further.

This chapter describes some of the ways in which tests are used. It is intended to provide some insight into the benefits of using tests. It reviews:

- using tests for selection
- using tests to promote self-understanding
- using tests for screening
- using tests for job analysis.

Under each of these headings the use of different types of test is examined. Only when we have a good idea of how tests are used, shall we be in a position to think in detail about whether using tests would be helpful to us in our particular situation.

Using tests for selection

Almost certainly the most widespread use of tests is in selecting people for jobs. However, it should be recognized that tests are rarely used alone in the selection process but are usually only one of a number of sources of information, including application forms, references and job interviews. Both ability tests and personality measures are used for job selection, although the reasons for using each of them should be different as they provide very different sorts of information about the applicant.

General ability tests

Tests of general mental ability are widely used for selection purposes. They are particularly appropriate for entry level positions where organizations are likely to have large numbers of applicants. In such settings, for example the recruitment of 18-year-old school leavers or university graduates, there is evidence that recruiting more intellectually capable applicants is likely to mean that the organization recruits more productive workers. (This evidence is discussed in Chapter 6.) What is most important at this stage is to understand the arguments for using these sorts of tests.

Organizations that do not use tests as part of their selection process are likely to say that they rely on other indicators. They take account of such things as educational qualifications as recorded on the job application form, interviews, and references as measures both of the suitability of the applicant for the job in question and to form an impression of the candidate's ability. The argument for using tests centres both on the weakness of these other methods for measuring ability and also on the advantage of having comparable data from all applicants. For example, although educational qualifications can give some insight into the knowledge and skills that applicants possess, in many cases applicants will have a variety of different educational qualifications which are difficult to compare. Even if two applicants have degrees in the same subject but from different universities, it is difficult to know whether they will have covered the same material in their courses or the extent to which standards at the two universities are comparable. However, if both applicants take the same standardized test, it is relatively straightforward to compare their test performances (see Chapter 5).

The main advantage of using a test of general mental ability is that such tests are usually highly reliable and valid, and therefore provide accurate estimates of applicants' overall ability. Some tests will provide a profile of ability, for example separate score estimates for verbal, numerical and spatial ability. It is straightforward to rank applicants in terms of ability on the basis of test results. Whether applicants are then selected solely on the basis of test scores, or whether test results are considered alongside other data about the applicants, will depend on a variety of factors, many of which may be situation-specific. In an ideal world an organization would have conducted a validity study (see Chapter 6) to find out whether test results alone are a better predictor of subsequent job performance than are test results combined with other information about the applicants. In practice, few organizations have the resources to conduct such studies and, as will be discussed in Chapter 6, some psychologists would question the extent to which such studies are necessary in the light of the considerable research evidence linking general intellectual ability to job performance.

There is, therefore, a prima-facie case for using tests of general mental ability in selecting people for jobs. However, the use of such tests is not entirely straightforward. Tests need to be reviewed to see whether they are likely to have an **adverse impact** on particular minority groups, that is whether some test takers will find a test more difficult for reasons not related to the test's ability to predict job performance. Tests also need to be of an appropriate level of difficulty for the applicant pool – neither too easy nor too difficult. This is particularly important as a test that is too easy or too difficult will fail to discriminate between applicants. On an easy test all applicants will tend to get high scores and on a difficult test all will tend to get low scores. In both cases it is likely that the **range** of scores applicants obtain on the test will be restricted and this limits the likelihood of the test successfully predicting their job performance.

Tests of special abilities

These tests are also widely used in selecting people for jobs. They may be tests designed with a particular occupation in mind, one example being a trainability test for sewing machinists, where applicants are given a demonstration and the opportunity to practise a simple task before being assessed on their performance of the task. Alternatively, they may be tests of the special abilities that are required for a particular job. A test designed to measure clerical aptitude might include a number of subtests, such as a test of speed and accuracy in checking for errors, a test of numeracy skills and a test of understanding written information. The main issue is then one of choosing the appropriate test for the specific occupation. In these circumstances, some evidence is required of the validity of the test for selecting people for the particular occupation. Choosing a test just because it claims to measure the particular special ability would be insufficient.

An organization also has to be mindful whether it is aiming to select those who already possess the necessary abilities (in which case it wants to measure proficiency) or those with the potential to develop the skill (where a measure of aptitude is required). (See Chapter 3.)

If there is evidence available supporting the validity of the test for the particular occupation for which it is being proposed, then the questions that need to be asked about the test are similar to those that apply to general ability tests:

- Does it have an adverse impact?

- Is it at an appropriate level of difficulty?

Tests in this category typically have similar reliability levels to general ability tests (see Chapter 5).

Measures of personality

Many organizations also use personality measures for selecting people for jobs. Their use in these circumstances is controversial. Many psychologists would argue that there is little evidence to support their validity for predicting subsequent job performance. There are a variety of reasons for this:

- Personality measures ask about preferences for particular activities rather than measuring ability to do the activity. Answering positively to the question: 'Do you enjoy being the leader of group?' is clearly different from demonstrating leadership ability.

- Personality measures are based on self-report. They are therefore much more liable to distortion by the applicant, either consciously or unconsciously, when they are being used for selection. If applying for a job as a bank clerk, how would you reply to the question: 'I double check for errors when I perform calculations – always; sometimes; never?' It is readily apparent that in these circumstances most applicants would perceive that there are right and wrong answers to the questions, even if the instructions for the test emphasize that there are no right and wrong answers.

- Personality measures sometimes use a particular type of forced choice question format of the kind: 'Would you rather work: a) on your own? b) in a group?' This is called an **ipsative** question and, for statistical reasons, scores from such questions cannot easily be used to make predictions in a meaningful way. This is because the alternative answers to the question are scored on two different scales of the test. On an ipsative test, as one scale score increases, another decreases. In statistical terms, the scores on the different scales are not independent of each other, so that as one scale's ability to predict increases others' decreases. (This is an area of considerable technical debate, see for example, Bartram, 1996; Closs, 1996; Baron 1996.) Tests using this question format can be useful in other contexts, such as for promoting self-understanding. Scores describe an individual's preferences for different sorts of activity or preferred personal style.

Some organizations that do use personality measures say that they use them not to make predictions about job performance but to give themselves additional information about applicants before they interview them. They may also suggest that personality information is useful in terms of predicting whether people will fit into the job, and their ability to get along with work colleagues. One situation where personality tests are useful is in screening people for emotional stability if they are are going to be working in high-stress, high-risk settings, such as in nuclear power stations or as security guards.

These uses of tests are justifiable if there is evidence to support them. However, it must be remembered that personality measures are usually less reliable than tests of ability. This means that the individual score estimates have more measurement error associated with them (see Chapter 5). This would be readily apparent to users if scores were typically reported as probable score ranges rather than as individual scores.

If a computer-based narrative report is being generated on the basis of a person's profile of scores from a personality measure, there are a number of additional questions that should be asked. The key question is: 'How has the report been validated?'

Most computer-based narrative reports are in fact based on modelling the interpretations of experts. The reports are, therefore, not based on validity studies (see Chapter 6) but on clinical judgements. The reports aim to describe how the person typically behaves. There are some advantages of using computer-based reports rather than relying on reports produced by individual psychologists. For example, a computer-generated report is always consistent. The same set of scores will produce an identical report every time. However, by definition, the computer has no other information available to it apart from that used to select the comparison group for score interpretation. It cannot therefore take account of any more detailed information that might be available about the person who has completed the personality measure. In contrast, an individual writing a report will almost certainly have access to other information about the person or the situation under which the personality measure was administered.

A second concern about computer-based narrative reports concerns their sensitivity to changes in the score profile. If anyone completes the same personality measure two days running, some of the scores will change; it would be very unlikely that in answering several hundred test items on two separate occasions someone would achieve an identical set of scores. Such changes should be considered as random error associated with the measurement process and not as any indication that the individual's personality has changed. In addition, we would also recognize that our mood will change from day to day. It is likely that some of the apparently random changes in test performance can be attributed to such minor mood swings. These are the practical difficulties facing anyone who has to interpret a score profile from a personality measure. If the interpretation is over-sensitive to small changes in test scores, it can be criticized for treating scores as if they had a spurious degree of accuracy. On the other hand, if people with similar, but not identical, scores get the same narrative report, the resulting interpretation can be criticized for failure to distinguish between applicants.

In addition, there are ethical issues to consider in the use of personality measures for selecting people for jobs. For instance, whether the content of the items in certain personality measures is an invasion of a person's privacy. In the United States, the use of some personality measures for job selection has been challenged in the courts for this reason. It seems intuitively reasonable to think that the items included in personality measures should be capable of being shown to be job related if they are going to be used in this way, but it is much harder to demonstrate this in practice.

Of most importance, however, is that when narrative reports are produced, there is a named and qualified individual to take responsibility for the content of the report so that, if and when it is challenged, there is someone to explain and justify the interpretation. It is, therefore, a matter of using test results responsibly.

Using tests to promote self-understanding

Arguably, the increased use of tests for promoting self-understanding is the most significant change that has taken place in testing practice. Although computers have made tests much easier to use and have certainly resulted in increased test use, the idea that test results can be communicated to and used by the person who takes the test represents a major shift in the model of testing practice.

However, one of the key issues if test results are to be used in this way is that test takers, who are in this case also the test users, need to be clear why they are taking the test. Essentially, this is about the person being tested being sufficiently well briefed by the person responsible for the testing that the test taker feels he or she is participating on the basis of having given informed consent to testing.

Interest inventories

Measures of occupational interests, vocational preferences and work values are widely used in careers counselling. These are measures that are based on many of the same assumptions as personality measures, where it is assumed that the individuals themselves are the best source of information for describing how they typically behave. Not surprisingly, interest inventories and other similar measures rely on self-report, for who else but the individual can say what their interests are?

Although these measures are constructed in a variety of ways and have different underlying rationales, they represent one of the most successful areas of psychological testing practice. One of the most well known interest inventories, the Strong Interest Inventory, has been described as one of the most researched psychological tests and is described in Figure 4.1.

These measures are used primarily to aid occupational exploration by helping individuals identify occupational fields that are likely to contain occupations that they will find interesting. They do this, typically, in one of two ways. In one, an individual's answers are compared with the answers of people working in a wide variety of occupations, so that for each occupation an individual gets a measure of how similar their interests are to those of people already working in the occupation. In the other, the inventory generates an individual score profile on a set of interest dimensions and the interest score profile is compared with the profiles obtained by people working in the occupations. Some measures, such as the Strong Interest Inventory (SII), combine both these approaches in a single questionnaire.

Most of us have only a limited knowledge of the range of jobs that exist even within our own occupational area. Consequently, the value of using measures of occupational interests, and related measures, applies both to individuals who do not know in which occupational area they want to work and to individuals who might have a good idea of potential occupational areas that are of interest to them.

Figure 4.1 The Strong Interest Inventory (SII)

Background: Men's form first published in 1927. Continuously revised, the latest revision was published in 1988.

Design: Originally used to compare an individual's scores with those from people working in different occupations. Now also incorporates scores on occupational themes, interest scales, an introversion/extraversion scale as well as administrative scales.

Items: The inventory has 325 items that ask about interests in a wide range of occupations, school subjects, leisure activities, contacts with different sorts of people, as well as self-descriptive statements.

Scoring: Five main sources of information: 106 occupational scales, 6 occupational themes, 23 basic interest scales, introversion/extraversion and academic orientation scales, plus scales to identify invalid or unusual profiles. It can be scored only by computer.

Use: Mainly for career counselling. Suitable for people of above average ability. Also used for helping people review their careers.

Research: Extensive longitudinal research has demonstrated the stability of interests and that people in occupations that fit their interest profile are more satisfied than those in occupations with poorer fit.

The goal of using an interest inventory or similar measure is not to identify a specific occupation but to learn about potential jobs in an occupational area and how they differ. The individual, with the help of his or her careers counsellor, will then need to find out more about specific occupations, such as their education and training requirements, before making a commitment to a particular career direction. A careers counsellor would also want to explore what other evidence exists to support the interest inventory results. This might be from hobbies and other outside interests, from subjects studied and so on. By doing this the careers counsellor is, in effect, looking for contextual information to support the test results.

At present these measures are primarily used with young people before they enter the labour market, that is when they are at school or university, although they can also be used effectively by career changers or people re-entering the labour market. Much careers advice is oriented towards making sure that people enter appropriate training, as nowadays there are relatively few jobs that can be entered without specific training. In these circumstances it is wise to make sure that any training course will lead to interesting work opportunities.

Measures of personality

Generating self-insight is also one of the prime reasons for using personality measures. In such circumstances, where the individual completing the measure is the main user of the test results, there is likely to be little reason to expect that replies will be distorted in any way. There is, therefore, an argument for using personality measures in circumstances where comparative information would be useful to an individual. Getting insight into how an individual's behavioural preferences compare with those of other people is likely to be helpful in many counselling situations, especially where the counselling is concerned with helping people deal with typical day-to-day problems.

In occupational settings, personality measures might also be used to give people insight into their personal style, for example to help them reflect on their preferred style of interacting with work colleagues. Sometimes such measures might be given to a work group or team, and individuals might share their results to promote a greater understanding of each other's work styles and preferences.

In career counselling with adults, the demand for advice is often as much about choosing the right setting as choosing the right occupation. Information from personality measures is often helpful to people in making such decisions.

One of the other main ways in which personality measures are used in work settings is in support of training and personal development. A measure of preferred learning style, for example, might be useful for an individual considering different training options, as in self-study versus going on a training course.

Tests of ability

These are also sometimes used for promoting self-understanding, especially in careers counselling. Being successful in a job is a function of both having the capabilities to do the job and having the motivation to do it. While measures of occupational interests can help with the latter aspect, in many instances there is also a need for people to get some measure of whether they already possess, or could acquire, the knowledge and skills that are required to do the job. Tests of general ability and of special abilities are relevant in this kind of situation. Information gathered from tests can then be evaluated along with other information that might be available, for example educational qualifications, work experience and so on.

Using tests for screening and diagnosis

Screening and diagnosis is the third area where tests are widely used. Many applications of testing fall under this heading and a wide variety of tests are used for these kinds of applications. Ability tests, for example, may be used to shortlist applicants for jobs, to identify children to refer for further assessment in a wide range of educational settings, by the courts as part of the process of deciding whether someone is fit to stand trial, and so on.

Many personality measures are also primarily designed for screening and diagnostic purposes, that is to identify those whom clinical psychologists should assess further and to assist in the development of appropriate treatment. Measures that are used for personality assessment range from simple checklists designed explicitly for screening, to measures that are designed to produce a more comprehensive personality profile. Figure 4.2 describes the Minnesota Multiphasic Personality Inventory (MMPI), one of the most widely-used measures in clinical assessment.

In addition to the use of many standard and widely-used tests, there are very many specialist tests and measures that have been developed for screening people in specific situations. These range from the symptom checklists that are widely used in healthcare settings, through sight and hearing tests, to measures designed for psychiatric screening.

Testing for screening purposes is widely used in schools and other educational settings. For example, many schools will administer a general ability test to all students in a particular year group. The results might be used by the school in a variety of ways. These include:

- the identification of children who seem to be under-performing in school, that is children who score well on the test but are performing less well in class

- the streaming of children by ability level for some subjects, or to ensure that classes contain a mix of children of different ability levels.

Schools also use specialist tests, for example of reading ability or verbal comprehension, to monitor progress of individual children in particular subject areas.

Figure 4.2 The Minnesota Multiphasic Personality
Inventory (MMPI)

Background: First published in 1942 and widely used since that time.
Revised edition MMPI-2 published in 1989. New form MMPI-A for use
with adolescents.

Design: Designed to use criterion keying where an individual's pattern
of replies is compared with those of people who have been diagnosed
as falling into certain clinical groups. Scores generated on eight clinical scales plus masculinity-femininity and social introversion as well
as three validity scales.

Items: Original version had 550 items answered on a True, False, or ?
New version replaced about 100 of these items.

Scoring: Test generates a profile of scores. Test interpretation now
based on pattern of high scores which are used to generate codes to
describe different profiles. Large number of special scoring procedures have been developed for the MMPI. Computer-based test interpretations available and widely used.

Use: Mainly by clinical psychologists in clinical assessment as
designed for clinical screening.

Spin-offs: California Psychological Inventory draws about half its items
from the MMPI but designed for use with the normal population.

Research: More than 5,000 published studies using the MMPI. Important indicator of extensive use and clinical experience associated with
its use.

Much assessment and testing is carried out for diagnostic reasons with
children and adults with learning difficulties. Most of this type of
assessment is carried out on a one-to-one basis using tests that have been
specially designed for use in these situations. Testing in these cases is used
to assist in the design of appropriate educational and training interventions.

Screening is frequently used to identify individuals for special treatment
or further assessment, and to allocate teaching resources appropriately
within a school or educational establishment. It can also be used to assist

in the allocation of resources between schools. For example, if one school is found to have a high proportion of children with reading difficulties perhaps it should be given an extra teacher who specializes in teaching reading skills.

Using tests for job analysis

One application of testing that is not widely known is the use of tests for **job analysis**. The analysis of what activities are involved in particular jobs is extremely important to organizations and it is relevant to a wide range of activities that organizations undertake. These include the selection and placement of new recruits; training and development activities; performance appraisal; organizational design; human resource planning; human factor issues in the use of computers and complex equipment; pay and reward. Psychologists and others have developed a variety of methods for analysing jobs. These range from observing people performing jobs to interviewing people about them. Interviewers often use what is called the 'critical incident' method to gather reports of particularly effective or ineffective behaviour. This is an approach to interviewing that asks the respondent to think of someone who performs the job excellently and goes on to ask them to describe one example of that individual performing well. The process is then repeated, only this time the respondent is asked to describe a poor performer and give an example of when they performed ineffectively.

Psychologists have also developed structured questionnaires to collect information about the work behaviours required in different jobs. These questionnaires can be considered to be psychological tests that are designed to identify the key knowledge, skills, abilities and other attributes that a job requires. They are designed to sample a wide range of these work attributes and to assess the extent to which they are required for any particular job. In this way they are designed to distinguish between jobs. The information generated should be relevant when selecting people to perform the jobs and identifying training needs.

Sometimes these questionnaires are designed to be given to people performing the job; others are designed to be completed by managers or supervisors. Typically, the questionnaires involve respondents completing checklists to identify the tasks involved in the jobs being assessed, as well as ratings of the overall importance of the tasks to the job. This might be in terms of the proportion of time spent doing the task, the importance of the task to the successful performance of the job, or the difficulty of performing the task effectively.

In practice, particular questionnaires are likely to be suitable for the analysis of different kinds of work. One of the first measures developed for job analysis was the Position Analysis Questionnaire (PAQ) (McCormick *et al.*, 1969). Measures developed in the UK include the Job Components Inventory (JCI) (Banks *et al.*, 1982) and the Work Profiling System (Saville and Holdsworth Ltd, 1988). These measures are based on a considerable amount of research and can be evaluated against the same psychometric criteria as other tests. Questionnaire-based methods are less frequently used for the analysis of managerial jobs.

Information from job analysis using tools such as these can be used to identify the tasks and skills required for jobs, to provide detailed job descriptions, and to rate the performance of job incumbents. As well as providing data that can be helpful in selecting people for jobs, job analysis also provides information that can be useful in the design of training programmes.

Key issues in job analysis are to recognize that:

- jobs change over time

- in many jobs the way it is done and what it involves is influenced by the job incumbent

- technological and organizational changes have a profound impact on the nature of jobs

- some jobs also have strong seasonal components.

One particular form of job analysis that increasingly affects many individuals is having their jobs evaluated for pay purposes. In practice, much of this kind of assessment relies on trained evaluators using expert knowledge. It often seems there is little evidence that such measures have the supporting information available (e.g. reliability, validity) that would normally be available to support the use of a psychological test.

It is important to recognize that job analysis is an approach to studying jobs and is not the same as testing job incumbents with conventional psychological tests that are then going to be used to select new job applicants. While getting job incumbents to complete selection tests is one way of collecting information to validate a selection test, it is not a technique of job analysis, although it might generate information on the ability requirements of a job.

Summary

This chapter has set out to review the main areas where tests are used. These are using tests:

* for selection

* to promote self-understanding

* for screening

* for job analysis.

Under each of these headings the main types of test that are used have been described, as well as some of the advantages and disadvantages of using them. Descriptions of two widely-used tests are also given.

Modern standards of good practice suggest that promoting self-understanding should always be one of the goals of using tests, as test results should always be communicated to the test taker.

5 Understanding test scores

If a child comes home from school and says, 'I scored 15 on the French test', the parent might ask, 'Out of how many?' The parent's response might well be influenced by whether the child says '20' or '60'. Whichever reply the child gives, the parent's next question might be: 'How did everyone else in your class do on the test?'

Test scores always need to be seen in context. Knowing that the child scored 15 out of 20 rather than 15 out of 60 may tell us something about the child's knowledge of French, but it might merely tell us something about the difficulty of the test. The parent's second question shows that the parent realizes that test performance is frequently best understood by comparison with the performance of others on the same test. If the child says, 'Mine was the second best score in the class', regardless of the possible total score, the parent is more likely to be satisfied with the child's performance.

Sometimes tests have a 'pass' mark, so another question the parent might have asked the child is, 'Did you pass?' The notion of passing or failing a test implies that a certain level of performance indicates a satisfactory level of competence. It might be taken to indicate mastery of the subject matter or a certain standard of achievement.

Understanding performance on a psychological test is no different from understanding performance on a classroom test. Normally, it is the relative test performance that is discussed. It is how the performance of one person on the test compares with that of other people that is of interest.

However, if a test is designed to measure the outcome of a training programme, for example the driving test, or an educational programme – the typical classroom test – there is frequently a pass mark. Achieving the pass mark in a test implies that some kind of prediction can be made regarding level of performance. In the driving test, it indicates a judgement about being able to drive safely; in the school test, it might indicate readiness to go on to the next stage of an educational programme; in employment, it might indicate competence to use equipment safely, or that a level of performance has been reached that merits promotion or a pay rise.

The approach to scoring based on the behaviour to be expected from someone with a particular test score is called '**criterion-referenced**' scoring. It can be contrasted to '**norm-referenced**' scoring, in which a person's test score is compared with those of an appropriately selected group of other people – the '**norm** group'. Sometimes the criterion-referenced approach to scoring a test is further distinguished from an approach to score interpretation called '**domain-referenced**'. Domain-referenced scoring emphasizes degree of mastery of the test content, for example what proportion of irregular French verbs are understood by a child with this level of performance on the test.

Most psychological tests use a norm-referenced approach to scoring, although the criterion-referenced and domain-referenced approaches to the interpretation of test scores are important in educational and training contexts. Even when a criterion-referenced or domain-referenced approach is used, it can be argued that a normative framework is implicit in all testing, regardless of how scores are expressed. The choice of content or skills to be measured will be influenced by the examiner's knowledge of what can be expected from people at a particular developmental or instructional stage. Saying that someone has passed a driving test implies a prediction that the person can now drive safely.

Norm-referenced scoring

The direct numerical report of a person's performance on a test, or scale of a test, is called their **raw score**. As noted above, this frequently has no, or only limited, significance by itself and can be sensibly interpreted only by comparison with some standard.

A raw score of 80 on a test of spatial ability does not represent twice as much ability as a score of 40. Psychologists have had to develop ways of talking about what they mean by 'equal differences' to compare the performance of one person with that of someone else. The development of scoring procedures for tests is an integral part of the measurement of individual differences (see Chapter 2).

Percentiles

The easiest way of comparing people is by ranking them. Just as the child's parent might ask 'How many people did worse than you?', so performance on tests can be evaluated by asking a revised version of the same question,

'What percentage of people did worse than you on the test?' The advantage of using percentages is that group sizes vary and using what is called **percentile** ranking gets round this problem.

The person who is ranked in the middle of the group, with half the group scoring below, is at the 50th percentile. This point is also known as the **median**, while the 25th and the 75th percentiles are called **quartiles**. The interquartile range is the difference in raw scores between the 25th and 75th percentiles and along with the median is used to give some measure of the distribution of scores. The method of calculating percentile scores is shown in Appendix Figure 1 (page 158).

The main advantages of percentile scores are:

- They are easy to explain to people who are not knowledgeable about statistics.

- Computation is straightforward.

- Exact interpretation is possible even if the scores are not normally distributed.

The main disadvantages are:

- They cannot easily be used for statistical analysis.

- They give no information about the actual difference in scores.

- They underestimate differences at the extreme ends of the distribution and overestimate differences at the middle.

In test manuals percentile scores are usually presented in tables with percentile scores as one of the axes and the raw scores associated with that percentile score plotted alongside. Separate tables will be provided for different norm groups (e.g. by age). Figure 5.1 shows a hypothetical example of a percentile score table for schoolchildren. The percentile score associated with a particular raw score can be easily read from the table. In this example girls consistently score higher than boys. So a child who has a raw score of 41 is at the 60th percentile for the total group, which means that 60% of children in this norm group have lower scores on the test. If that child is a boy, he has scored at the 70th percentile compared with other boys. On the other hand, if that child is a girl, she has scored at the 30th percentile compared with other girls. This example shows how in the middle of the score range a small difference in score can lead to a large change in the percentile score. Similarly, a raw score of 44 is at the 70th percentile for the group, 75th percentile for boys and 50th percentile (the

Figure 5.1 Percentile score table (hypothetical example)

Percentile	Raw Scores – Boys	Raw Scores – Girls	Raw Scores – Total
99	63 plus	70 plus	66 plus
95	58-62	62-69	60-65
90	53-57	58-61	55-59
85	48-52	53-57	50-54
80	46-47	51-52	48-49
75	43-45	49-50	46-47
70	40-42	47-48	43-45
60	37-39	45-46	41-42
50	36	44	40
40	34-35	42-43	38-39
30	32-33	39-41	36-37
25	29-31	36-38	33-35
20	25-28	31-35	28-32
15	20-24	25-30	22-27
10	13-19	17-24	15-21
5	6-12	11-16	9-14
1	5 or less	10 or less	8 or less

median) for girls. On the other hand, a raw score of 58 is at the 90th percentile overall, 95th percentile for boys and 90th percentile for girls. In this case the percentile score is very similar whichever reference group is used. It can be seen from the table that people at the middle of the distribution are concentrated over a narrow range of raw scores, while people at the extremes have a wider range of raw scores.

A test manual may contain several sets of tables of this type. Each table will be for a separate norm group. For example, there may be a separate norm table for each year group of children, norm tables for college students, the general population, and so on. The test user has to decide which norm group to use for comparison purposes when wishing to interpret and compare percentile scores for a particular group of people who have taken the test.

Standard scores

Francis Galton, the 19th century British scientist, was the first person to suggest that a person's test score could be described by the amount that the individual's score differed from the average score for a group of people.

Figure 5.2 The normal distribution

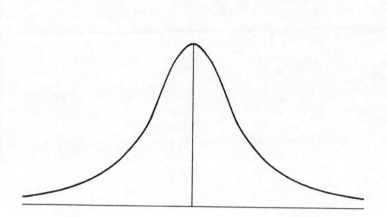

Nowadays it is very common to summarize the performance of an individual in terms of the number of **standard deviations** that the score differs from the **mean** of the group with which the person is being compared. In everyday terms the mean is the arithmetical average. The standard deviation is a measure of the spread of scores and can be thought of as a measure of the average deviation from the mean. (It is actually the square root of the average squared deviation from the mean.)

Standard score systems are based on the fact that we find that many human attributes are distributed on a normal or near-normal distribution. The **normal distribution** is the symmetrical bell shaped curve, which is the frequency distribution that would be obtained for a long series of chance events, such as a large number of people tossing a coin fifty times and recording the number of heads. Figure 5.2 shows the shape of this distribution.

If the scores on a test are normally distributed, 68% of test takers will score within one standard deviation of the mean and 95% within two standard deviations. Only 5% of test takers will score outside of this range, which means that only 2.5% score more than two standard deviations above the mean, while exactly the same percentage will have scores more than two standard deviations below the mean.

Standard scores show how far individuals' raw scores deviate from the mean for the group with which they are being compared by converting the raw scores into proportions or multiples of the standard deviation. An example showing how to calculate the standard scores from the mean and the standard deviation of a set of scores is shown in Appendix Figure 2 (page 159).

Using standard scores has a number of advantages when the distribution of raw scores is approximately normal:

- Differences in standard scores are proportional to differences in raw scores.

- When used in calculating averages or correlation coefficients (see Figure 5.6), standard scores give the same results as would come from using raw scores.

There are some disadvantages to standard scores:

- They are more difficult for the non-expert to understand because of decimal points, negative scores, and small numerical range.

- They are not suitable if the scores are not normally distributed.

In practice, the use of standard scores is convenient when the distribution of test scores is approximately normal. This does not mean that most psychologists believe that the normal distribution is some sort of natural distribution for human characteristics.

Standard score systems

For statistical analysis, the mean of a standard score system is set at zero and a person's score is expressed in terms of the number of standard deviations they score above or below the mean. However, when presenting test scores psychologists have preferred not to deal with negative or decimal scores. They have, therefore, developed a number of other common standard score systems. In these systems, which are summarized in Figure 5.3, the mean and standard deviation (SD) are set in such a way as to eliminate negative or decimal scores.

It is to some extent confusing that different test developers have chosen to report scores using a variety of different standard score systems. However, in practice most test users work with a relatively small number of tests and soon become familiar with the standard score systems used.

Figure 5.3 Standard score systems

Percentile score for normal distribution	z score Mean 0 SD 1	T score Mean 50 SD 10	Deviation IQ Mean 100 SD 15	Stanine Mean 5 SD 2	Sten Mean 5.5 SD 2
	-4 SD	10			
1	-3 SD	20	55		
2.5	-2 SD	30	70	1	1.5
16	-1 SD	40	85	3	3.5
50	0	50	100	5	5.5
84	+1 SD	60	115	7	7.5
97.5	+2 SD	70	130	9	9.5
99	+3 SD	80	145		
	+4 SD	90			

Common standard score systems are:

T Scores – A widely used system which has the convenience of avoiding negative scores and decimal points.

Deviation IQ –This is the scale used for reporting IQ (intelligence quotient). It should be noted that some tests use a standard deviation of 16 rather than 15. This scale is still used for some tests that have dropped the term 'IQ' because of its unwarranted developmental assumptions.

Stanine – Stanine (meaning Standard Nine) was introduced by US Air Force psychologists in World War II. The scores run from 1 to 9, thus providing a single digit system of scores. One standard deviation is two scale points. Stanines 1 and 9 are open-ended.

Sten – Sten (short for Standard Ten) is used in the Sixteen Personality Factor (16PF) questionnaire developed by Cattell. It is similar to the Stanine system but with a mean of 5.5.

Relativity of norms

The normative approach to scoring and interpretation is used by most tests. To understand test scores that are reported using either percentiles or a standard score system, it is important that the norm group that has been used for interpreting scores is recorded. When choosing an appropriate norm group from a test manual it can be difficult to decide which sample is most nearly equivalent to the people being tested. When using non-UK norms, test users need to be especially careful that they understand the terms used to describe different sample groups. For example, many US tests will describe samples by grade in the US education system, or use terms such as 'freshman' or 'sophomore' to describe college student groups. If a test is being used regularly for the same purpose with a particular sample group, such as university graduates, constructing local norms would clearly be worthwhile and is relatively straightforward to do using a spreadsheet, or similar program, on a computer.

Other score systems

There are a number of other scoring systems used by some tests. The three described briefly below are the more widely used alternatives to percentiles and standard score systems.

Raw scores – A few tests are designed to be interpreted using raw scores. The Self-Directed Search, a widely used interest inventory is one well-known example.

Age- or educational level – Some tests use age- or educational-level scoring systems, for example, scoring a child's performance on a test as being like that of an average 6-year-old. These are commonly used for tests of educational attainment and for some tests of general mental ability designed to be administered to children. They are condemned by many experts on psychological testing (e.g. Cronbach, 1990) as being prone to misinterpretation. This is primarily because they are really rank order and not interval scales – the difference in test scores between children aged 8 and aged 9 will not generally be the same as the difference in test scores between children aged 5 and aged 6.

Ipsative scores – These are obtained from tests that use a forced choice question format, typically interest or values inventories, or personality questionnaires. These tests aim to compare the relative preference of one individual for different activities, and not the overall level of preference of that individual for the activities compared with other individuals. Ipsative scoring is a system for ranking an *individual's* scores. Its usefulness is based on the assumption that it can be more important to know someone's strongest preference than how that preference compares with those of other people. On an interest inventory, this might mean finding out that a test taker's strongest preference is for working with people and the lowest for working with things. If the test taker is making a choice between different work options it does not matter that other people typically score higher or lower. What is important is for the test taker to be clear about his or her preferences.

This approach to test construction has some advantages. For example, it offers ways of examining the consistency of a person's preferences. However, as already noted in Chapter 4, there are difficulties in using such a scoring system to make predictions. Some tests combine ipsative and non-ipsative question types.

Criterion-referenced testing

This is an alternative approach to scoring and interpreting tests. Instead of – or as well as – comparing how a person stands in relation to other people who have taken the test, it translates the test score into a statement about what to expect of someone with a particular test score. Results on an arithmetic test might be used to show that a child is better than 80 per cent of their age group and to state that the child is competent at executing certain specific arithmetical operations.

In classroom and training contexts this approach to scoring and interpretation is popular because it focuses on the level of performance rather than using what sometimes seems to be a competitive or comparative yardstick for evaluating performance.

Expectancy tables

Test scores may be interpreted in terms of expected performance. An **expectancy table** is one way of presenting the information, and shows the probability of different outcomes for persons who obtain particular test scores. Figure 5.4 shows a hypothetical example of an expectancy table.

Such a table could be used to predict that someone with a particular class of degree will be earning within a specified salary range five years after graduation. It implies that a follow-up study has collected the required data. It is, therefore, one way of presenting the results from a criterion-related validity study (see Chapter 6). This is a form of **actuarial prediction**. In many practical situations, outcomes can simply be divided up into 'success' and 'failure'.

Measurement error

All measurement has error associated with it, and psychological test scores are no exception. If someone took the same test two days running or

Figure 5.4 Example of an expectancy table

Degree class	No of cases	Percentage in salary range 5 years after graduation		
		less than £15,000	£15,000-£20,000	over £20,000
First	133	5%	25%	70%
Upper second	476	9%	37%	54%
Lower second	354	20%	52%	28%
Third	105	32%	63%	5%
Pass	59	41%	56%	3%

completed two versions of the same test that were meant to be equivalent, it would be surprising if they obtained the same score. While it might be surprising if their scores changed considerably, a small change is to be expected and can be attributed to chance or random factors that affect day-to-day performance.

However, if the same test was taken for a second time six months or a year after it had first been taken, a larger difference in scores would not be surprising. The problem would be in deciding how much of the change should be attributed to random changes in performance and how much should be attributed to changes that have taken place in the individual in the intervening period. For children, it is natural to assume that performance will change over time as they grow up, but even here there are problems in deciding whether changes are being measured reliably by the test. Errors in measurement could lead to real changes being under- or over-estimated.

Chance **errors of measurement** associated with a particular test can have important consequences and, if they are large, limit the usefulness of any decisions based on the test scores. In such situations, scores obtained on the test could not be considered dependable and it would be foolish to make predictions from them. Reliability may be defined as 'the extent to which the outcome of a test remains unaffected by irrelevant variation in the conditions and procedures of testing' – in effect, the degree to which test scores are free from measurement error.

Measurement error can come from a range of possible sources. It may be from the person being tested, who might be more or less anxious, better motivated, or more tired on one occasion than the other. It may be from the situation in which the testing is taking place, or that events immediately prior to testing affect the performance of the person taking the test.

Increasingly, psychologists are recognizing that performance is affected by the interaction of the person and the situation.

Once it is as accepted that all test scores have measurement error associated with them there are two important practical consequences. It becomes necessary to:

- *Identify sources of error*: There is a responsibility for the test developer to report information about known levels of measurement error for the intended uses of the test. This usually means collecting a variety of forms of evidence that can be used to estimate measurement error, and hence the degree of reliability of the test. Typically, this would include information on the reliability of different forms of the same test, changes in the level of performance that might be expected over time and so on.

For the test user concerned with choosing a test that will be reliable in a particular situation, this involves evaluating the data that should be provided by the test developer in the test manual. This is discussed in more detail below.

- *Treat scores as estimates*: Too often test scores are treated as fixed immutable characteristics of people. In fact, all test scores are estimates that are based on a sample of behaviour – the test. For this reason there is measurement error associated with all test scores. There is a need for a fundamental change in how test scores are reported. Instead of reporting a single score, a better practice would be to report the probability that someone's score on a test is within a certain range, the **confidence interval**, of the actual score obtained on the test.

If test scores were routinely produced in this way, test users – the main consumers of test results – would quickly realize that some tests allow more precise estimates than others. Short tests are usually less precise than longer ones; personality scale scores are usually less precise than ability scale scores. With computers taking much of the strain out of test scoring, there is little excuse for test scores not being reported like this.

Already, some computer-scored tests routinely produce test scores in this way. It is particularly important for tests that produce a profile of scores to be presented as a score range rather than as a set of specific scores. One scale may have a higher test score than another but, if the confidence interval of scores for one scale overlaps with that of another scale, there is the possibility that if the person was tested again the order of the scores might be reversed. Some tests now print percentile score bands to demonstrate that it is the probable score range that should be evaluated, not the precise score. Because this error range is calculated in terms of raw

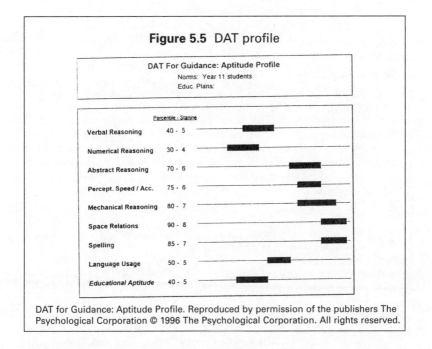

Figure 5.5 DAT profile

DAT For Guidance: Aptitude Profile
Norms: Year 11 students
Educ. Plans:

Percentile - Stanine

Verbal Reasoning	40 - 5
Numerical Reasoning	30 - 4
Abstract Reasoning	70 - 6
Percept. Speed / Acc.	75 - 6
Mechanical Reasoning	80 - 7
Space Relations	90 - 8
Spelling	85 - 7
Language Usage	50 - 5
Educational Aptitude	40 - 5

DAT for Guidance: Aptitude Profile. Reproduced by permission of the publishers The Psychological Corporation © 1996 The Psychological Corporation. All rights reserved.

scores, the exact percentile range it will cover varies according to the percentile score obtained, tending to be greater around the median than at the extremes of the distribution.

Figure 5.5 presents an example of the score profile that is obtained with the Differential Aptitude Tests (DAT). Not only are the percentile score and stanine obtained on each test reported but also the **standard error of measurement**, so that for each test there is a score band. In this example, when score bands overlap it should not be assumed that one score is higher than another. On re-test we would expect the test scores to change but to stay within the bands.

How to evaluate the reliability of a test

For someone who has to interpret test scores the reliability of the test would be readily apparent if the test scores were reported as probable score ranges. Unfortunately, this is not how most tests report their scores. Test users, therefore, have to seek out information from the test manual on the reliability of measurements carried out with the test.

In most test manuals information on the reliability of the test is reported as the **correlation** obtained between one set of test scores and another. Figure 5.6 describes the correlation coefficient.

Figure 5.6 The correlation coefficient

The correlation coefficient is the statistic that describes the strength and direction of the relationship between two sets of scores. Correlation is expressed on a scale of -1.00 to +1.00. A score of 0.00 indicates no relationship and a score of 1.00 a perfect relationship, where the distribution of scores from one measurement is exactly the same as the distribution from the second measurement. The sign in front of the correlation coefficient indicates the direction of the relationship. A positive score means that as scores on the first measure increase, so do scores on the second measure. A negative score indicates that as scores on the first measure increase, scores on the second measure decrease.

It is important to remember that correlation coefficients are estimates, and as such are subject to error. In practice, the meaning attached to the correlation coefficient will depend to some extent on the sample size, that is the number of people for whom there are data available.

The most common ways of measuring the reliability of a test are:

- Correlations between **alternate forms** of the same test. These might be from two equivalent forms of the test administered at the same time, or two forms administered at different times.

- Correlations between scores on the same form of the test administered at different times. This is often referred to as test-retest reliability.

- Correlations between scores from half the items on the test with scores from the other half. Frequently referred to as 'split-half' methods, these methods are used to estimate reliability from a single administration of the test.

It is clear that these different ways of measuring reliability are in fact estimating different sorts of error that can be associated with the testing process. Sometimes these three methods of calculating reliability are given different names. Correlations between alternate forms of the same test are called coefficients of **equivalence**, correlations between the same test administered at different times are called coefficients of **stability** and correlations from split-half methods are described as coefficients of **internal consistency**.

Each of these ways of identifying the measurement error associated with using a particular test can be important to the test user. Comparing scores obtained from alternate forms of the same test administered at the same time measures the degree of similarity of the item content. If the same test is administered after a period of time has elapsed, the stability of what is measured by the test is being assessed. Methods based on evaluating the internal consistency of a set of test items are important for determining the extent to which the test items can be considered to be measuring the same thing. Normally a test manual provides some information about these three aspects of reliability. In some cases, additional information might be provided. For example, if a test relied on the person administering the test making judgements to score the test, the correlations between the scores given by two different administrators to the same set of replies would be a measure of scorer reliability.

It is reasonable to ask what reliability levels are typically observed. Correlations between two forms of the same test administered at the same time might be 0.9 or higher. In general, correlation coefficients measured in this way should certainly be above 0.8.

The correlation between two sets of scores for the same test, where the same people have taken the test at time 1 and again at time 2, will tend to decrease as the time interval between the first test session and the second increases. In some circumstances, change is to be expected and low reliability would not give cause for concern. While interest inventory scores would be expected to show high reliability, scores on a measure of depression might not. Test manuals frequently report correlations that have been obtained over a variety of time intervals. Correlation coefficients might range from 0.8 or higher over a short time interval (a week, a month) to 0.5 or less over a year.

In evaluating the levels of reliability that are reported in a test manual, it is important that the sample size, that is the number of people who took the test, is reported – a sample size of 30 is the minimum acceptable. In general, the larger the number of people in the sample the more accurate the estimate of reliability will be. Correlation coefficients are subject to measurement error in exactly the same way as test scores.

It is important to realize that reliability is a function of both the people who took the test and the test itself. It is not sufficient to know that a test is reliable for the intended application without knowing that it is reliable for the intended target population. The test manual, therefore, should give information on the nature of the subject groups on which the reliability of the test has been measured.

The level of reliability that is required for a test to be useful will also depend on the purpose for which the test is being used. Tests being used to assess individuals need to be more reliable than tests being used to screen groups of people. For example, a shorter test, which will usually be less reliable than a longer test, may be suitable for screening but not for individual assessment. The type of test being considered will also affect the typical levels of reliability that are reported. Tests of maximum performance usually have higher reliability coefficients than measures of typical response. Correlations over time and between different forms of a test are usually higher for tests of maximum performance than for measures of typical response. However, with children we would normally expect scores on ability tests to improve rapidly over time as they develop, so that such test scores would be expected to change over time.

Summary

This chapter has examined how tests are scored and the main ways that test scores are reported. Key points to note are:

- Test scores are usually interpreted in relative terms, that is in terms of the performance of other people who have taken the same test (norm-referenced) or the standard of performance that might be expected from someone with a particular test score (criterion-referenced).

- Two main ways of presenting norm-referenced test scores are as percentiles or using a standard score system.

- It is important to be aware of the nature of the norm group with which the test score is being compared and its appropriateness to the context in which testing takes place.

- If a test is being used regularly with a similar group of test takers, test users should consider constructing their own norm tables.

- All test scores have error associated with them and it is important that the extent of error associated with scores from a particular test is recognized.

- Reliability is the term used to describe the extent to which test scores are free from errors of measurement.

- Best practice is to report scores as probable score ranges, with the actual test scores indicated as a point in the score range.

6 How to judge tests

While we obviously want to use psychological tests that give accurate measurements, that is to use more reliable rather than less reliable tests, we also want to know what these tests are measuring. This is called test **validation** and is at the heart of the process of evaluating psychological tests.

This chapter starts out by examining how psychologists approach test validation. It is important to understand this process because much of the data that are reported in test manuals and test reviews are based on studies of this kind. The first part of this chapter is concerned with the answer to the question: 'How do I know if this test is worth using?' Part of the answer to the question was given in the previous chapter. The test is worth using if it is reliable. However, it must also measure something useful.

The next sections of the chapter present information to answer the questions: 'Should I use the same tests as everyone else?' and 'Will it be worth it?' They are concerned with how we generalize findings from particular studies to the use of tests in a wide range of settings and whether there are economic arguments that can be used to justify test use.

The final sections of this chapter examine the issues concerned with making sure that testing is carried out fairly. These remind us that the context in which tests are to be used also has to be considered when we make judgements whether to use tests or not. The influence of social and cultural factors on test performance should not be underestimated.

Test validation

The validity of a test is generally defined as the extent to which the test measures what it is intended to measure. It is the most important consideration in the evaluation of any test. Validity can be considered as a measure of usefulness. It implies the question: 'Useful for what?' The validity of a test cannot be measured in general terms but only in respect of the particular use for which the test is being considered. We need to review the evidence for the validity of a test in deciding whether or not to use it.

It is important to recognize that a variety of inferences may be made from scores produced by a given test. It is appropriate to suggest that we do not validate tests, but rather validate the inferences we wish to make from our knowledge of test results. The Standards for Educational and Psychological Testing (AERA/APA/NCME, 1985) stress that validity is a unitary concept that 'refers to the degree to which ... evidence supports the inferences that are made from the scores.'

There are two broad dimensions to the measurement of validity which are reflected in two questions:

- How well does the test predict the performance in which we are interested?

- What does the test *really* measure?

These questions raise two very different types of measurement issue. The first question focuses on the **criterion**, that is the standard against which the success of a test's predictions will be judged. It is about seeking to establish a relationship between test performance and that standard. The second question focuses on the test and enquires about the underlying theory or psychological constructs the test aims to measure.

Purpose determines the method of validation used for a particular problem. Is the problem about using the test performance to predict performance on the criterion, or is it about investigating the content or constructs that a test actually measures?

Cronbach (1990) stresses that validation is about enquiry. Different approaches to validation imply different types of enquiry. However, different approaches to validation should not be seen as equivalent alternatives that can substitute for each other but rather as approaches that complement one another. Three broad approaches to validation are explained below. These are called **criterion-related validity**; **content-related validity** and **construct-related validity**.

Criterion-related validity

A prime concern in applied 'real-world' settings is the extent to which test results predict how people are likely to perform in other situations. Performance on the test is checked against some external criterion that is a direct and independent measure of what the test is designed to measure.

Typical examples might be:

- comparing the score on an aptitude test with subsequent job performance

- comparing the score on an extraversion scale in a personality measure with ratings of a person's typical behaviour from friends or work colleagues.

Several assumptions underpin this approach to test validation. The first is the notion of stability. The implicit assumption is that how individuals behave in one situation is related to how they behave in other situations. The second assumption is that two test takers with the same score are predicted to behave in the same way.

When talking about criterion-related validity, it is usual to distinguish two approaches:

- **predictive validity**: when tests are used to make predictions about the future

- **concurrent validity**: when tests are administered to diagnose existing status, or when criterion data are already available.

One distinction between these is in terms of a time dimension. If the criterion is measured at the same time or is available when the test data are collected, the process is concurrent validation; if the criterion is measured at some time after the test data have been collected, the process is predictive validation. However, the logical distinction between predictive and concurrent validity is based not on time but on the objectives of testing. This can be seen by comparing the two questions:

- Is the test taker under stress? (Concurrent validity)

- Is the test taker likely to become stressed? (Predictive validity)

Sometimes a measure of concurrent validity is used as a substitute for a measure of predictive validity. This might occur because it is not practical to allow the necessary time to elapse in order to conduct a predictive validity study. Test and criterion data might be collected from existing job incumbents to validate the use of a test for selection.

The problems and pitfalls associated with the measurement of criterion-related validity become clear when the stages involved in collecting such data are examined. These are summarized in Figure 6.1.

Figure 6.1 Stages in a predictive validity study

1 **Specifying the situation for study** – For an organization, this might be trying to predict future job performance in order to measure the success of a training programme. In an educational setting, it might be selecting students for a course.

2 **Agreeing an appropriate criterion** — Both client and investigator have to agree on the criterion. In occupational settings, job performance is often evaluated by supervisor or manager ratings. In a school or college, exam results might be seen as an appropriate criterion.

3 **Setting the time-scale for the study** — Will ratings of job performance be made after six or twelve months? Will exam results after the first year of an educational course be used or should exam results at the end of the course, that might not be available for two or three years, be used?

4 **Agreeing the sample** — The test might be given to existing workers, new recruits or entrants on to a course who have already been selected. By definition, applicants who were not selected are excluded.

5 **Administering the test** — The test might be given prior to collecting performance data, at the start of the course or at the end of training.

6 **Collecting criterion data** — It is important that the measures of criterion performance are collected completely independently of the test data.

It is clear that a criterion-related validity study takes a considerable amount of time to carry out. Only when all the aspects of the design have been agreed and the data collected (which may take a year or more), can the analysis be carried out to see if the test data actually predict performance.

Specifying the criterion

The most difficult part of the design of any criterion-related validation study is the specification of what will count as suitable criterion data. A common criterion measure is the rating or grade given by some 'expert' judge. For example, a manager or supervisor might rate job performance.

There are many obvious weaknesses with these sorts of data. They include:

- Do the judges know the relevant facts about the individuals they are rating?

- To what extent do ratings merely reflect the quality of personal relationships between the individual and the judge, who might be a work supervisor?

- Would different judges give the same ratings, that is how reliable is the criterion measurement?

A general problem with criterion measures is ensuring that their measurement is independent of test performance. Knowledge of the test score can act as a self-fulfilling prophecy when judges are subsequently asked to make ratings. This is an example of a process often referred to as **criterion contamination**.

Key issues, therefore, in the choice of an appropriate criterion are:

- Whether the criterion can be measured reliably.

- Whether the criterion measure is a valid indicator of what is being predicted.

The relationship between test and criterion

Normally a positive relationship between test score and criterion performance is expected. For example, a higher test score would be expected to be associated with better job performance and vice versa. If a statistically significant, but negative, relationship were obtained, that is if a low test score was found to be associated with better job performance when a positive relationship was expected, this would indicate that the psychological test could be used to predict criterion performance but that the theory underpinning the prediction would have to be questioned.

Whenever a validation study is carried out there are several key points that need to be borne in mind.

- When making statements about the validity of a test for a particular purpose, the sample of subjects used for the study will obviously affect the nature of the population about which any generalizations can be made. For example, if the test has been used to predict school performance by testing secondary school students and comparing performance on the test with examination results, it would be unwise to assume that the same test will necessarily predict exam performance for university students.

- It is also important that subjects participating in the study do vary in terms of test and criterion performance. A restriction of range in the distribution of either test or criterion scores will result in a change in the validity coefficient. The statistical strength of the relationship between two variables will decrease if the **variability** of either of them decreases.

- The reliability or measurement error associated with the test score and the criterion performance also act as limiting factors in determining the maximum possible relationship that can be obtained between the test and the criterion scores. It is, therefore, particularly foolish to spend a lot of time developing a test and then use an unreliable criterion measure in a validation study.

Practical aspects of decision-making using tests

The decision about whether to use a particular test in a given situation is also influenced by many other factors besides criterion-related validity. Other factors that affect the decision to use a test in a particular situation include the **selection ratio**, the **base rate**, the **forecasting efficiency** of the test itself and the cost of testing. Judgements about differences between sets of test scores are also influenced by **effect size**. It is important to understand the effect these have on the use of tests in real-life situations.

In order to look at these in greater detail, we will use as an example the relatively simple decision of whether or not to offer someone a job on the basis of their test score. If we had previously conducted a predictive validity study we would be able to plot on a graph the test scores that individuals had obtained before their appointment against their subsequent job performance (the criterion). For convenience, rather than plot the individual data points, we draw the ellipse that would contain all the individual data points. This is called a **scattergram** and Figure 6.2 shows an example of one.

We would have to decide on the level of job performance that we would consider satisfactory. Figure 6.3 presents the same scattergram, only this time we have determined that those scoring above a certain score, shown by the horizontal line, perform satisfactorily on the criterion, that is job

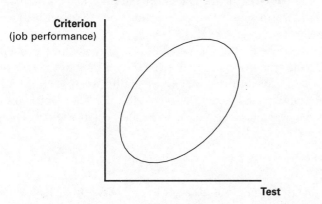

Figure 6.2 Example scattergram

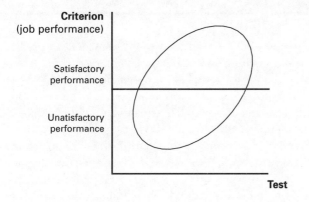

Figure 6.3 Scattergram with satisfactory and unsatisfactory criterion performance determined

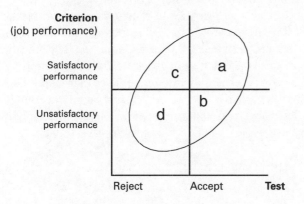

Figure 6.4 Scattergram with cut-off score

performance. This level of performance on the criterion distinguishes those judged to perform satisfactorily from those judged to perform unsatisfactorily.

In practice, if we were selecting people for a job, our next decision would be to decide what level of test score we would require before we offered a job. This is called the **cut-off score** and Figure 6.4 shows what our scattergram might look like once we had selected it. The scattergram is divided into four segments which have been labelled a, b, c and d. These can be defined as:

a – people who had satisfactory job performance and who would have been accepted on their test scores

b – people who performed unsatisfactorily but who would have been accepted on their test scores

c – people whose job performance was satisfactory but who would have been rejected by the test

d – people whose job performance was unsatisfactory and who would have been rejected by the test.

It is then possible to think about the accuracy of the test scores for predicting criterion performance. Groups a and d have had their criterion performance correctly predicted by the test. They are sometimes called '**hits**'.

Groups b and c have not had their criterion performance correctly predicted by the test and are sometimes called '**misses**'. Group b are sometimes called '**false positives**' and group c '**false negatives**'.

The more 'hits' and the fewer 'misses' there are, the more useful the test would be at predicting criterion performance. In fixing the cut-off point for a selection procedure, we want to select a level of test performance that maximizes the numbers in groups a and d and minimizes the number in groups b and c.

The numbers in the different cells of the figure will be determined by the correlation between test performance and the criterion, and by the proportion of the group who are judged to perform successfully on the job. It is possible that in different circumstances different values would be attached to the 'false positives' and 'false negatives'. In selecting people for jobs, we might be more concerned about false positives than about false negatives, preferring not to take on people who would be unsuccessful in the job and being less concerned about not taking on some people who could have done the job successfully. In some screening situations we would be more concerned about missing people – the false negatives – than accepting some people unnecessarily for further investigation – the false positives.

Selection ratio

The selection ratio is the proportion of applicants that are offered a job. As Figure 6.4 illustrates, it can be expressed as (a + b)/(a + b + c + d), that is the number of people who are judged to perform satisfactorily on the test divided by the total number of people who took the test. In practice, we find that a test of low validity will still be useful if the selection ratio is high, that is if there are a large number of applicants for every place. In this case we would be able to raise the cut-off score on the test and still have enough applicants to fill any vacancies. We would not worry that we would miss a large number of potentially satisfactory performers. Conversely, a test of high validity would be of little benefit if the selection ratio is low, where nearly every applicant is being offered a job. In that situation we would probably be selecting a significant number of people who were subsequently found to be unable to perform the job satisfactorily.

Base rate

The base rate is the proportion of people in the population under study who exhibit the characteristic being measured by the test. When tests are being used for screening purposes, it is possible to distinguish two types of error that one might make on the basis of test scores. False positives are people identified by the test as having the characteristic but subsequently found not to possess it (people in quadrant b in Figure 6.4), while false negatives are those not identified by the test but who actually have the characteristic (people in quadrant c in Figure 6.4).

The usefulness of a test for identifying people with the characteristic is influenced by the number of people it will identify as false positives and false negatives. If the condition being tested for is very rare, and therefore has a low base rate, even a highly valid test will identify large numbers of false positives if applied to the general population. In this case the cut-off score will have to be set sufficiently low to make sure there are no false negatives if the screening process is not to miss people whom it is designed to identify. As a result, many people who do not have the condition are likely to be mistakenly identified by the test. However, the test may be useful if the base rate is higher for the target population to whom the test will be administered. For example, patients attending a stress clinic or counselling service might be more likely to be suffering from stress than people in the general population.

Forecasting efficiency

One way of evaluating the predictive validity of a test is in terms of the percentage reduction of error that would be obtained from using a test of known validity for the decision being made. The higher the correlation between test and criterion, the greater the reduction; this is called the forecasting efficiency of the test. It is a measure of the extent to which using a test improves prediction over just guessing.

A correlation of about 0.3 between test and criterion improves forecasting efficiency by about five per cent, a correlation of about 0.6 improves it by about 20 per cent and a correlation of about 0.9 improves it by about 70 per cent. These may appear quite modest gains considering that most predictive validity studies achieve correlations between 0.3 and 0.6. However, it does mean that using a test is better than picking people at random.

Cost of testing

The decision whether to use a test will also be influenced by the cost of testing. Obviously, the lower the cost of testing the more likely it is that the benefits will outweigh the costs. However, calculating costs without taking into account benefits is not very sensible. The cost of testing is a function of the amount of testing required to obtain the desired outcome. This will be affected by the numbers that have to be tested. For screening purposes the number will be affected by the base rate, and for selection purposes by the selection ratio. It is also a function of the validity of the test. A test that has higher validity for the decision being made will be more efficient at making correct predictions – hits – and consequently reduce the number of misses. It will therefore produce greater benefits from the same amount of testing. Only when testing is very expensive, as in some forms of medical screening, are costs likely to outweigh the benefits of testing. The economic benefits of testing are discussed in more detail later in this chapter (see page 88).

Effect size

Very often we are interested in comparing the scores from different groups of people. Do girls score better than boys on reading tests? When we find a mean difference of five score points between the performance of boys and girls on a reading test, with girls on average obtaining a higher score than boys, it is difficult to evaluate this figure on its own. It is useful to look at the size of the difference in relation to the standard deviation of all the scores obtained. The ratio of mean difference to standard deviation is called effect size.

In this example, if the standard deviation (s.d.) of the scores obtained by the children who took the test is 10 score points, the mean difference is 0.5 s.d. – that is the effect size is 0.5. If the standard deviation were 5, the effect size would be 1.0. A mean difference of 0.5 s.d. would usually be of practical value and suggests that there is a difference in the scores of boys and girls on this test. This does not mean that all girls score better than all boys. There is a need to be aware of incorrectly stereotyping people because of their group membership. If scores on a test are normally, or approximately normally, distributed, the range of scores (maximum to minimum) will be at least 6 standard deviations. Boys who score one standard deviation above the mean for all boys are also scoring better than most girls on this test.

Content-related and construct-related validity

Besides using tests for practical prediction purposes, we frequently want to identify the *concepts* that a test measures. Both content-related validity and construct-related validity are concerned with the concepts underpinning a test. They can be distinguished in terms of the purpose for which these two approaches to measuring validity are used.

Content-related validity is most readily understood by considering the problems in constructing a test of achievement. The test is validated by the extent to which the test items accurately reflect the aspects of the competence being assessed. Therefore it is necessary to specify very carefully the precise subject area (usually referred to as the content domain) that the achievement test is to assess. For example, in a test designed to measure language skills we need to identify what specific skills the test will be designed to measure: vocabulary, appropriate use of grammar, writing skills, and so on. Once the content domain has been decided, test items have to be generated to represent each of the various aspects. The items are then tried out on a sample of people, and their difficulty (in terms of the proportion of people giving correct answers) assessed.

Content validity involves both logical analysis of the content domain and statistical analysis of how the items worked in practice. The final selection of items for the test would be based on the outcomes from these kinds of analysis. Content validity is built into a test by the selection of representative items from the content domain in the process of test construction.

Construct-related validity is the analysis of the meaning of test scores in terms of psychological concepts or 'constructs'. To interpret what a test measures in psychological and scientific terms, it is necessary to understand the concepts that determine the test scores. Interpretation of a psychological test is built up gradually and is probably never complete. Over time, a more complete understanding is obtained of the factors that affect the test performance and the strength of their influence. At present theories of abilities, interests and personality are incomplete, so the interpretation of even the most well-established and researched psychological test will be short of ideal.

Whereas criterion-related validity is examined in particular settings, construct-related validity is only established through a long interplay between observation, reasoning and imagination. Four main ways of assessing construct-related validity have been identified (Hood and Johnson, 1991):

- **convergent validity** – evidence of similarity between scores from a particular test and scores on other tests designed to measure the same construct

- **divergent validity** – evidence that scores on a particular test are not related to scores on tests known to measure other unrelated constructs

- **internal consistency** – the extent to which items in a test, or from a particular scale on a test, associate with each other and with the total score on the test or scale

- **treatment validity** – the extent that the results from a test can be shown to be relevant to decisions about a person's treatment.

Face validity

Readers will also come across the term **face validity**. This refers to whether a test looks appropriate for its intended purpose, but not whether it *is* actually appropriate. It is important to distinguish face validity from content validity. Face validity is concerned with the apparent relevance of the content of the test for the decision for which it is being used and not whether the content of the test can be shown to be relevant to the decision in question. However, the apparent relevance of the test is important because, if a test does not appear relevant for the purpose for which it is being used, this may undermine its actual use.

What does this mean in practice? A reading test designed for semiliterate adults would probably be inappropriate if the items were carried over from a test for children. It is highly probable that the test would lack credibility with the adult population and this might well affect the degree of seriousness with which adults would complete it. The lack of face validity of the test in this particular situation might well mean that in such circumstances the results from testing had more measurement error associated with them – their practical value having been undermined by the apparent inappropriateness of the test content.

However, face validity is never a substitute for other evidence of test validity. Even if the test did contain items that were judged appropriate, it might still be inappropriate for use because of other factors, such as test scores not predicting reading ability. Face validity on its own is no guarantee that a test is satisfactory to use in a given situation.

Validity generalization

Recently there has been considerable debate among psychologists about whether it is necessary to conduct predictive validity studies for every situation in which a test is used. Conventional wisdom was that the validity of tests was situation-specific and that a test should not be used just because it had been shown to be useful in another, apparently similar, situation.

To most users of psychological tests this was to counsel what seemed like unobtainable perfection. There are numerous practical difficulties in adopting this approach. These include:

- the time it takes to conduct a proper predictive validity study where individuals are tested at selection and then have their job performance measured at some later time

- the difficulty of running two selection procedures in parallel

- the unreliability of many measures of job performance limiting the strength of relationship that can be found between the test scores and the criterion measure

- the problems of following up only those who have been employed and not being able to follow up those who have not been employed

- the small sample sizes available for many such studies, meaning that whatever relationship was found between test scores and subsequent job performance would be subject to considerable measurement error.

Faced with these difficulties it is not surprising that many people who were using general ability tests for selecting people for jobs took what appeared to be a more pragmatic approach – they used tests which they believed would be valid for their specific situation on the basis of the availability of validity data when the test was used in a similar setting. In practice this usually meant that users were relying on validity data reported in the test manual.

The main difficulty with this approach is that it rests on several assumptions. First, there is an assumption that the jobs or situations being compared are similar in terms of content and performance requirements and, secondly, there is an assumption that the test takers in these different situations are similar in terms of ability range as reflected in the pattern of test scores they obtain. Although conventional wisdom was that these risks were not worth taking, the degree to which practice followed professional opinion was limited. In part this was because many users felt that using a well constructed test would almost certainly mean that their selection process would be of higher quality than if tests were not used. For example, provided tests were properly administered they would at least offer a standardized procedure for assessing applicants.

The emerging consensus is that what many people were doing in practice perhaps was not so wrong after all. It is important to understand the reasoning on which this is based. It is argued that successful job performance is related more to general ability than to special abilities. As a direct consequence, this means that general ability tests are the best sort of tests to use for selection as they are the best predictors of job performance. From this it also follows that once a test has been shown to be a valid predictor in one situation then it can safely be used in other similar situations.

This approach to understanding predictive validity is called **validity generalization**. It is based on what is called the method of **meta-analysis**. Meta-analysis is a method for cumulating the findings from many separate research studies to provide a more accurate estimate of the relationship between test scores and job performance. In psychology and other social sciences the problem of measurement error, when studies are completed on relatively small numbers of people, is always considerable. This is why I have argued in this book that test scores should always be reported as a probable score range rather than as a single test score. In the same way, measures of the relationship between test scores and job performance should also be treated as estimates that will be more or less accurate. Accuracy of estimates will be influenced primarily by sample size, but also by the reliability of both measures (test and measure of job performance) and by the range of scores obtained by subjects on the two measures.

Meta-analysis sets out to use correlation coefficients, which are a measure of the strength of relationship between two variables, from different studies in combination, taking into account the fact that sample size will vary across studies. In this way it calculates a more accurate estimate of the correlation coefficient between the test and job performance. This estimate is more accurate because effectively it is based on the combined sample from all the studies. It can also be used to calculate corrected correlation coefficients that take into account measurement error and **range restriction** in test scores or criterion performance.

Meta-analysis is not only an important technique for test users but is also important as a way of cumulating research findings in general. Policy makers often complain that for every study that shows there is a relationship between two variables (for example poverty and ill health), there is another that contradicts this finding. Meta-analysis can be applied to research findings that seek to address public policy and evaluation issues, that is studies that seek to answer questions of the form: 'Do programmes of this kind work?'

However, although meta-analysis has had a major impact over the last decade and has changed psychologists' views on validation studies, there are a number of important qualifications that need to be borne in mind in interpreting the results of meta-analysis studies:

- There are situations where tests of special abilities add significantly to prediction, or predict better than tests of general ability.

- Relying on a single test of general ability is not necessarily the best approach if we are making placement decisions. Using two different tests where we are trying to allocate individuals to different jobs is likely to locate a greater number of satisfactory workers.

- Psychologists do not in general believe that jobs differ only in terms of their general ability requirements.

- When applicants are of similar ability levels (e.g. graduates) it is the contrasts, that is whether somebody has high spatial ability or high verbal ability, that are most likely to be of interest.

It can be argued that by integrating results from a large number of studies it is not surprising to find that one significant relationship dominates. On the other hand, no one giving careers advice would advise people to consider themselves suitable for jobs on the basis of general ability alone. Most of us would recognize, for example, that we possess verbal, numerical and spatial abilities to varying extents and that these abilities are more or less relevant to particular types of work. The education and training system also filters people progressively over time. People with poor numerical skills are unlikely to study maths and science or to end up applying for jobs as engineers. Motivation, interests and personality are all clearly relevant as well. The challenge for psychologists and others is to conduct well-designed research studies that demonstrate this.

However, there is no doubt that the arguments for validity generalization and meta-analysis are attractive to employers. As jobs in many organizations seem to be changing almost constantly, employers might argue that what they want are people who can be trained quickly to acquire new skills and to take on new roles and responsibilities. Measures of general ability would seem to be particularly attractive in such circumstances, notwithstanding the arguments outlined in the preceding paragraph. On the other hand, it seems reasonable to suggest that people with specialist knowledge and skills will be equally important to organizations because of the unique added-value they will offer; it is harder to argue that they should be selected exclusively on the basis of general ability. People with experience of selection will also recognize that you can over-select, that is choose somebody who is too well-qualified for the job. Such people are likely to get bored and leave if they do not find the job challenging.

Perhaps the main danger from an uncritical acceptance of the validity generalization argument is that it encourages the indiscriminate use of tests. While it is clearly impractical to argue that tests ought to be validated in every possible situation in which they might be used, the idea that all use of tests will be valid is also seriously flawed. The important practical issues involved in choosing tests and using them properly are discussed in Chapter 7.

It is important to note that, while psychologists disagree about the use of validity generalization, both sides would agree on the poor quality of many small-scale validity studies. Cronbach (1990) notes that, 'Statistical integration of results from weak studies is an interim attempt to "make do." Better studies, particularly studies with better criteria are much needed.'

Economic benefits

What are the benefits of using psychological tests? As far as using tests for personnel selection is concerned, organizations want to know the economic benefits of using tests. However, these can be manifest in several different ways. For example, does a selection procedure reduce:

- training time?

- number of failures during training?

- labour turnover?

These should be easy to calculate and they imply economic benefits through direct savings of time and recruitment effort. However, using a more valid selection technique should also result in an organization employing people who will be more productive. For example, if under the old selection procedure staff in a financial setting handled an average of 100 transactions a day and staff selected under the new procedure average 120 transactions a day, there is a clear economic benefit.

In practice, several factors influence the benefit that will be obtained from using a particular test for selection purposes. These are the validity of the test, the selection ratio, the extent of individual differences in job performance and the financial benefit from small increases in production. It is important to understand how these factors interact with each other.

There is a natural tendency to want to be able to evaluate validity coefficients and to say that a test needs this level of validity to be useful. In practice, as we have already noted, even a test of high validity (above 0.5) will not be useful if the selection ratio is low, that is when nearly all of the applicants are being offered employment; and a test of lower validity (below 0.3) would be useful when many applicants are chasing few job opportunities (i.e. the selection ratio was very high).

The interrelationship of test validity and selection ratio can be related to job performance. Consequently the financial benefit, in terms of increase in productivity, resulting from using a test with a certain validity and a known selection ratio, can be calculated. While it is easy to understand the principle that improving a selection procedure results in economic benefit, calculating the extent of the financial benefit requires several assumptions to be made.

To estimate the full financial benefit it is necessary to value the increase in productivity that will result from using a test of known validity with a specific selection ratio. The technique for doing this is called **utility analysis**. Making some assumptions, it is possible to calculate for a given selection ratio and with a test of known validity, by how much productivity should increase. This is done in two stages. First, the productivity level obtained by the average worker before the selection test was used is calculated. Next the productivity of the average worker who has been selected under the new procedure is calculated. The difference between the two is then expressed in terms of the effect size, that is the number of standard deviations increase that is obtained from using the selection procedure. The outcome of this calculation might be that using the selection procedure would increase the average productivity level by, say, 0.7 standard deviations.

The next step is to calculate what this increase in productivity is worth. For many years this was seen as a major stumbling block, and apart from a few examples in textbooks the value of increasing average productivity was rarely calculated. However, on the basis of an extensive range of studies, it is now the convention to assume that one standard deviation of productivity is worth 40% of salary for the job in question. This rule-of-thumb approach suggests that if, for example, a position attracted a salary of £20,000 per year, the value of one standard deviation of performance is £8,000 per year.

In our example, therefore, the financial benefit would be £5,600 (0.7 x £8,000) per person per year selected by the improved selection procedure. It is important to remember that there are also some costs that have to be set against these estimates. These might include:

• additional costs of the new selection procedure that are incurred as upfront costs

• costs that arise because more productive workers will incur extra costs (e.g. consume more raw materials, expect higher wages)

• benefits not achieved if some good applicants are put off by the new selection process.

The net benefit received would therefore be somewhat less. There are also other assumptions being made, one of which is that the job does not change when more able employees are selected. However, if, in addition to the benefit of employing more productive workers, labour turnover was reduced, the organization would see additional financial benefits through not incurring extra recruitment costs.

What is clear from these arguments is that there are significant financial benefits to be made by organizations employing better selection procedures. Some writers have tried to gross up the productivity gains that could be made by the economy as a whole by using better selection procedures. While it is appropriate for an individual employer to make calculations on the basis of selecting people for jobs, for society as a whole it is allocation decisions that are being made. The greatest benefit will be obtained by getting people into jobs where they can make the greatest contribution, not by selecting the best and discarding the rest.

Fairness in testing

One of the key issues that concerns people about any testing procedure is fairness. The notion of fairness as applied to testing can be considered to have several components. The two main components of any consideration of fairness are:

• fairness of outcome

• fairness of process.

The concept of fairness applies particularly to the use of tests for selection, but it is really a concern for any decision based on test results. When children are allocated special needs assistance with reading, schools should also be concerned about the fairness of the procedures used because the children chosen are being allocated additional help while others are not.

In an ideal world not only would the testing process be fair but the result of testing would lead to a fair outcome. In practice we assess fairness by trying to determine how well the testing process measures up against this ideal.

Fairness of outcome

Where assessment is concerned, fairness of outcome is really measured by the reliability and validity of the testing process, that is the accuracy of the information that is generated by testing. It is measured, therefore, both by the absence of measurement error and by the validity of the test for the particular decision that is being made.

Measurement error, as measured by the reliability of a test, sets an upper limit on the observed validity of the test. The higher the reliability coefficient the better. However, high reliability, which implies low measurement error, is only the first prerequisite for achieving a fair outcome. It does not a guarantee that the outcome of testing will be fair.

Overall, fairness of outcome is dependent on the validity of the test for the decision being made. The higher the validity, the fairer the outcome is likely to be. However, it is not possible to guarantee a fair outcome without perfect validity. A higher validity coefficient merely increases the probability that the outcome will be fair. The fairest outcome in a particular situation is achieved by maximizing this probability.

In selecting people for jobs, fairness of outcome implies choosing the best person for the job. 'Best' being defined here as the person who is most likely among those tested to achieve the highest level of job performance.

In turn, this is dependent on there being some way of defining and measuring job performance. If the method chosen to define and measure job performance is, for example, ignoring certain features of the job, or is unreliable, then we have a poorly-defined criterion for 'best'.

Fairness of outcome is, therefore, primarily defined by technical aspects of the test and by the procedures used to validate the particular use of the test. It is a function of both the test and the processes used to measure the criterion. If these processes are of poor quality, then fairness is reduced regardless of the technical merits of the test.

Fairness of process

While the quality of outcomes is important, most of us would also be concerned that the processes used to achieve those outcomes are fair as well. This is really similar to saying that we want people punished who are guilty of crimes but we want them to have a fair trial, because we can only be sure they are guilty if they receive a fair trial.

However, a fair process does not necessarily guarantee a fair outcome. Tossing a coin would appear to be a fair process but certainly does not guarantee fair outcomes. It is just a way of making a decision where the outcome is determined by chance. It is only 'fair' in so much as each possible outcome has an equal chance of occurring and no one outcome is favoured. Nobody would want the outcome of a criminal trial to be decided in this way.

So what do we mean by a fair process when we are talking about psychological testing? In technical terms, one process could be defined to be fairer than another if there was less **systematic error** – what is normally called **bias**. Systematic error in testing can be contrasted with the random or chance errors that will inevitably occur in any testing process. While we want to minimize both types of error, it is the bias introduced into testing by systematic errors that will make the testing process less fair. So it is the systematic errors that need to be minimized to make the testing process as fair as possible.

In practice, if a systematic error in testing affects everybody's test scores equally, it is not causing bias, but is a source of **constant error**. Fairness of process is concerned, therefore, with systematic errors that affect people being tested to varying degrees, that is where some people's test scores are affected more than others.

While all measurement and, therefore, all testing has error associated with it, insomuch as this error can be considered to be due to chance effects, it can be quantified and treated as a margin of error associated with the measurement process and the results it produces. We deal with this error by referring to the standard error of measurement associated with a test score and by defining a range within which the test score probably falls (See Chapter 5).

Bias, which we can now define as systematic error that affects some test takers more than others, has the effect of depressing or enhancing the test scores of some people taking the test. (Note that bias also has a technical meaning in the item analysis of ability tests.)

What are the possible sources of systematic error that reduce fairness? They are numerous, but the main ones are:

- poor test administration

- inappropriate test choice

- test takers' expectations.

Poor test administration We have already noted that testing involves an attempt to collect data that are 'objective' by administering a test in a systematic and standardized way. We know that this is an unattainable ideal but it works reasonably well in most circumstances.

In reality, poor test administration occurs if specified procedures for test administration are not followed. It can also occur from inconsistencies in practice and when the person administering the test is not sensitive to context.

Inappropriate test choice The most obvious way in which a test can be inappropriate is by being too easy or too difficult for the applicants. Not only will measurement error be increased in such circumstances, but the reduced distribution of scores also limits the usefulness of the data for making predictions. Systematic errors are also likely to be introduced, for example because of the uncertain effect that sitting a very difficult test is likely to have on the test takers' motivation.

Tests can also be inappropriate for social or cultural reasons. This might be for language reasons, as for example, when a test written in standard English is given to people whose first language is not English, or the complexity of the language used for the test instructions itself acts as a barrier to test takers. If using an American test in the UK, it is especially important to look out for words that have different meanings or whose meaning may not be clear.

There are other social and cultural reasons that can make a test inappropriate. For example, there might be bias in favour of men if mechanical ability is tested by items based exclusively on car mechanics.

Tests might also produce biased results if test items make stereotypical assumptions, for example describing women as homemakers, or if they contain pictures or diagrams featuring few people from ethnic minorities in a multiethnic or multicultural society.

However well such an inappropriate test is administered, it cannot mitigate the test's inappropriateness or the consequent systematic error that is likely to be introduced into the test scores of some test takers.

Test takers' expectations   The hidden agenda of test administration is concerned with managing the test takers' expectations of the testing session. We all know that the style or way in which instructions are given can vary, and that as a result the way that the message is perceived will vary regardless of content.

Test takers also come to testing with varying expectations of the process. While these cannot necessarily be changed, they are perhaps more likely to be an issue in large-scale testing programmes where little attention is given to the individual test taker. Other factors that can cause bias include scoring errors. Although rare if tests are being computer-scored, unusual or atypical scores should always be checked.

Perhaps the biggest danger is to forget that testing takes place in a context. We tend to assume that the test performance is purely a function of the test taker. Actually test performance is a function of a person in a situation.

It may seem that I have pointed out a large number of reasons why testing may not be fair, but it is important to be aware of the limitations of testing if it is to be done as fairly as possible. In many respects fairness is an ideal concept and to some extent what matters is the relative fairness of the process.

While some activities clearly undermine fairness, if we are making a choice between one procedure and another the question is really which one is fairer. One argument for using tests is that it is easier to judge when testing is unfair than for many other assessment procedures. Such procedures are often more subjective in the way they collect information and in the way they make judgements on the basis of that information. They are even less likely to be fair but are also more difficult to challenge as being unfair.

Selecting fairly

Tests are used as part of the selection process for many jobs. Clearly, there are 'equal opportunities' concerns about the whole selection process and all its components, not just the use of tests. A few key points about evaluating selection procedures from an equal opportunities point of view are listed below. They apply to all aspects of a selection process and not just to the use of tests.

Monitor the performance of different groups Unless data are collected to record key facts about applicants, further analysis is impossible. Employers who wish to call themselves equal opportunities employers need to collect data routinely to monitor all aspects of their selection procedures, both internal and external. These data can be used to look at success rates of different groups at various stages of a selection process.

Policy on setting cut-off scores In Britain, quotas and positive discrimination in favour of certain groups (such as women or members of ethnic minorities) are not allowed. Selection processes are intended to treat all groups the same. This means using the same cut-off scores for all groups, even if this results in adverse impact.

Adverse impact If some groups are less successful than others, then the selection process can be seen to be having an adverse impact and should be reviewed: is the selection rule valid for all groups? Evidence to show the selection process is job-related and valid should be collected. In the UK selection processes have been ruled unlawful where they cannot be demonstrated to be job-related. Using a particular test could be inappropriate if performance on it is influenced by skills that are not required in the job.

If a process is found to have adverse impact, this may reflect genuine group differences, but other explanations should be also investigated. Do groups differ in other ways, for example in terms of educational qualifications? Are there particular aspects of the present selection process that disadvantage some applicants? Can these be changed without undermining the validity of the process? Would a different selection process be fairer, yet equally valid?

More employers are realizing the need for their workforce to reflect the diversity of society as a whole. If selection processes impede this, they need to review them.

Summary

This chapter sets out the issues involved in how we judge whether or not psychological tests are useful in practice. These include:

- Outlining the two main approaches to test validation and discussing how these are related to the purpose for which the test is being used.

- Distinguishing between predictive validity and concurrent validity as two approaches to criterion-related validity.

- Specifying the stages in a typical predictive validity study and noting the importance of having a reliable and valid criterion measure.

- Reviewing practical aspects of using tests for decision-making. This includes the effect of the selection ratio, base rate, forecasting efficiency, cost of testing and effect size.

- Describing content-related and construct-related validity and how they are evaluated.

- Outlining the argument for cumulating the findings from validity studies using meta-analysis.

- Reviewing the economic benefits that accrue from improving selection procedures.

- Discussing the issues involved in achieving fairness in testing and distinguishing between fairness of outcome and fairness of process.

- Examining issues involved in using tests for selection and, in particular, stressing the need to monitor all stages of any selection process, not just the use of tests.

7 How to use tests properly

For testing to be effective it must be carried out properly. In the preceding chapters we have reviewed why and where tests are used, and we have discussed many of the issues that affect proper test use. In this chapter we examine the practical issues that confront both the test user and the test taker when tests are used. The chapter reviews the main stages in any testing process and sets out what test users and test takers need to know for test use to be effective. We begin with the reasons for testing.

Why test?

Perhaps the most obvious question that someone who is being asked to take a test might raise is: 'Why am I being tested?'

First, it should be clear that the test user needs to have good reasons for using tests. This means being clear how the information from the test session is going to assist in decision-making. The different types of decision that information from tests can inform were discussed in Chapter 2. The reasons for testing will vary, just as the types of decision for which the test results will be used vary.

If a test is being used for selection it should be because the test is known to predict performance and to be fairer than other ways of making that prediction. If the test is being used in counselling or for careers advice, it should be because more objective assessment through testing is likely to generate information that will be helpful to the test taker and the counsellor or careers adviser. In schools tests are frequently administered both to provide more objective information about individual students and to monitor the performance of groups of students as a whole.

In the past it was often assumed that whether or not the test taker understood the reasons for testing did not really matter, provided the test user knew why tests were being used. The job seeker might be told: 'Well, if you want to be considered for this job, you have got to take this test (and

---

Figure 7.1 Reasons for testing

The test user should be able to explain to the test taker(s):
1. why they are being tested
2. what will happen to the test results
3. how feedback will be given.

---

by the way, don't expect to be told the result).' The counsellor might say, 'This will help me understand you', an equally unsatisfactory explanation.

It would be nice to think that such situations no longer occur. The byword for good practice in testing is 'informed consent', that is that the people being tested know why they are being tested, and agree to it. Explanations should cover not only why testing is taking place but also what is going to happen to the test scores and how the test takers will be given feedback on their test performance.

Although it should always be possible for the test user (or the person administering the tests) to answer these questions, the purpose of testing is likely to influence the decision that the test takers make about whether or not to take the tests. In selection situations, not taking the tests will almost certainly mean the applicants have excluded themselves from being considered for the job, so there is strong pressure to take the tests. In other situations, where the main purpose of testing is to promote self-understanding, the decision to take the tests is normally a joint decision of the test takers and their counsellors or careers advisers, for example. For children it may be the parents who make the decision on behalf of their child, although the purpose of testing should always be explained to the child. Clearly, with older children the decision process has to be negotiated with the child as much as with the parents.

How to prepare

A second question that test takers often ask if they know they are going to be tested is: 'How should I prepare for the test session?' This is an area where people can be given differing advice. The basic point that is frequently overlooked is that the test takers' degree of familiarity with the testing process will almost certainly vary and this is likely to affect their test performance. Unless this issue is addressed, the testing process will not be as fair as it could be and, by implication, some test takers may be disadvantaged because of this.

The issue of preparation applies mainly to tests of maximum performance, where the lack of familiarity of some test takers could lead to them achieving lower scores on the test than would be the case if they were more familiar with the testing process.

However, even measures of typical response, such as interest inventories and personality measures, can be stressful for some test takers and this needs to be recognized. Furthermore, if these types of test are being administered as part of a battery of tests in a selection process, test takers may also be concerned that there are right and wrong answers to any test, even if its instructions say that there are not.

The 'Guide for test takers' to be found at the end of this book gives more detailed advice and also includes example test items. It aims to be a self-contained source of information for people who might be asked to take a test.

Most tests of ability have always included a small number of example questions that are administered and explained to applicants before they start the test. The purpose of these items is really to relax the test taker and to orient them to the specific test they are taking. When taking a test myself, I once completed the practice items by finding the next item in the series. Only when the test administrator checked my answers, did I realize that I had been asked to identify the *next but one* in the series. It may be a silly mistake to make but at least I made it only on the practice items. I went on to follow the instructions very carefully in the rest of the test!

Practice items are all very well for people who are familiar with taking tests. Most people who have only recently come out of the educational system, who have just left school, college or university, fall into this category. For people who have not taken tests for a long time, or have not been educated in Western countries, this familiarity should not be taken for granted. Many organizations using tests on a large scale as part of their selection processes have now realized that they need to do more to make the testing process fairer to all applicants. This is particularly important where tests act as 'gatekeepers' to subsequent stages of the selection process.

Test publishers and employers have recognized the need to provide a pre-testing orientation to potential test takers. Typically, they have prepared explanatory booklets on why testing is taking place, describing the test content, giving example items and so on. These can be sent out to brief people who are being asked to take part in testing. Ideally, there should also be a telephone number or the name of a person who can be contacted to answer any additional questions that people might have about the testing process.

At least one test publisher has also published practice tests, a series of short tests which can be used to give candidates the opportunity to complete a test under real time limits. Practice tests are designed to simulate a real testing session and can either be sent out to candidates to complete at home, as they come with full instructions for self-administration and self-scoring, or be administered formally by an employer or careers adviser to help individuals prepare to participate in a selection process where ability tests will be used.

Such initiatives are to be welcomed. They certainly help to make testing fairer by removing gross inequities that might occur because of differing levels of familiarity with testing.

However, there are two other issues that also need to be addressed that are more controversial. First, there is the question of test-taking strategy, for example what should we say to someone who says: 'Should I guess if I don't know the answer?' Secondly, there is the issue of coaching in test taking, and practising taking tests. What effects do these activities have on test performance?

There is much general advice on strategy that can be given to test takers. Frequently it is assumed that this sort of knowledge is picked up in school or college, but often the advice that people receive is not good. Figure 7.2 summarizes some points to bear in mind when taking ability tests.

When tests are timed, it is important to attempt as many questions as possible, so it is better to omit items found difficult and come back to them later. On computer-administered tests, however, it may not be possible to go back to an item, so every question must be answered and a good strategy for guessing is important. Often it is possible to improve your chances of guessing the right answer by ruling out answers that are obviously incorrect. Even if incorrect answers are going to be penalized, this strategy for guessing would be worth following. However, guessing correctly can become a problem. One student of mine reported on taking an adaptive test: 'I didn't know the answer so I guessed. I got it right so then I got an even harder question and had to guess again!'

In the United States where standardized tests are used for entry to many universities, at both undergraduate and postgraduate level, coaching people for these tests is a business in its own right. As a result there has been considerable discussion and research on the topic. When most children in Britain had to take the eleven-plus examination, there was a similar debate. Today there are books available that set out to help people to prepare to take tests (see 'Guide for test takers').

People and books that claim to be able to coach people to take tests must be evaluated with care; the evidence suggests that the quality of

---

Figure 7.2   Advice for test takers

1. Give careful attention to test instructions
2. Work quickly
3. Answer, even if not absolutely certain
4. Guess, if uncertain
5. Review your answers

---

coaching is variable. However, good coaching can lead to significant improvements in test scores. The more significant question is about the impact of coaching on the fairness and validity of the testing process.

If only some test takers have access to coaching, coaching must undermine fairness. It also lowers validity because those who are more test-sophisticated score better than they would on the basis of knowledge of test content alone. If some test takers have access to coaching that improves their test scores, clearly that affects any decision made on the basis of those scores.

The pressure to seek out coaching is obviously greatest when a test is being taken at some particularly important decision-point. In Britain many children were coached for the eleven-plus examination because it appeared to have crucial educational consequences. It is perfectly rational to seek out coaching in such a situation. Cronbach states that 'If coaching specific to a test is prevalent, something is wrong with the system' (1990, p86). People develop at different rates and there is no one right age for sorting people into categories or educational streams. Overly selective systems are, in effect, merely rationing life chances by controlling access to educational resources or jobs.

Choosing a test

If testing is going to take place, an appropriate test must be chosen. The detailed information that needs to be reviewed, such as **test catalogues** available from publishers, is discussed in the next chapter. Here we are concerned with a number of more basic issues.

The decision being made

The type of test to be used is largely determined by the type of decision being made. In selection, a measure of maximum performance is likely to be used; for promoting self-understanding, measures of typical response are likely to be used as well.

In some selection situations, tests are administered in order to screen applicants. Only applicants who score above a certain level will be admitted to subsequent stages of the selection process. While this is not inappropriate, test users should be aware that it could have important implications for equal opportunities (as discussed in Chapter 6).

If it has been decided to use a measure of maximum performance, the next choice is between whether it is more appropriate to use a test of general mental ability, or a measure of special ability, or both. The precise nature of the decision being made will probably be the deciding factor.

The target population

Tests are designed with different people in mind. For measures of maximum performance, the most obvious dimension that needs to be taken into account is the difficulty level of the test. However, measures of typical response are also designed for different target groups. For example, the Strong Interest Inventory is an American inventory designed for people with, or aspiring to, a college education. It is unlikely to be suitable for use with 16-year-olds leaving school with few educational qualifications.

Issues of face validity also apply to the choice of tests. If the test lacks credibility with all or some of the test takers, this is likely to affect their motivation to take the test. Consequently, a test designed for children should not be given to adults and vice versa.

Information about the target population that a test is designed for is usually available in test publishers' catalogues. More detailed information is likely to be included in the test manual or reviews of tests (see Chapter 8 for a list of sources of information).

From a measurement perspective, difficulty level is a crucial factor with measures of maximum performance. Choosing a test that turns out to be too difficult or too easy for the people who are asked to take it means that the testing is largely a waste of time. The range of scores that people obtain will be restricted – all low scores if the test is too difficult and all high scores if the test is too easy. This lowers both the reliability of scores and their predictive validity. Technically, this is referred to as **attenuation**.

However, in some screening situations, tests with these characteristics are desirable. It is the very small number of applicants with high or low scores that the test is trying to identify. It does not matter that the vast majority of people who take these tests obtain very similar scores. What is important is that the scores of the small number of people that the test is trying to identify are well distributed, so that it is possible to set a clear cut-off score to identify with confidence those who should be followed up.

Individual or group testing

The choice of test will also be influenced by whether testing is being carried out with a group of people or with an individual. While some tests can be administered only to individuals, many more tests can be administered just as easily to a group as to an individual. Typically, these are paper-and-pencil multiple-choice tests, although increasingly these tests are also available in computer-administered versions as well.

Most tests that are designed only to be administered to individuals require the test user to have a high level of skill in using the test. On the other hand, many group tests are relatively straightforward to administer either to a group or to an individual. Often the test user will delegate the administration of the test to someone else, who should be trained in test administration and always be working under the supervision of the qualified test user.

Choosing a test appropriate to the individual test taker

The question here is about the extent to which the choice of tests can be influenced by the individual test taker. In selection situations the choice of test will be governed by the predictive validity of the test for the decision being made, regardless of whether it is being administered to one person or ten. While individuals may score high or low on the test, scores from a large number of candidates should exhibit a well distributed range.

On the other hand, if the test is being used to promote self-understanding, the choice of test will be geared to the needs of the individual. Other information about the individuals, such as educational records or information on their personal circumstances, must be considered in choosing which tests to administer. Making someone take a test that they will find very difficult and score poorly on is rarely, if ever, appropriate in such circumstances. Although the decision to test may be a joint one between the test taker and the test user, it is the test user who is expected to have the knowledge to select the appropriate tests.

Inappropriate test choice

The most serious constraint on test choice is probably the test user's limited knowledge of available tests. Inappropriate test choice is one of the most common areas of test misuse (Eyde *et al.*, 1988). However, it is not the case that the test user should bear all the responsibility for this, as it is often genuinely difficult to obtain impartial advice on tests or testing (but see Chapter 8). Difficulties can arise because some test users will be qualified to use only a limited range of tests. If their choice of potential tests is restricted it is possible that, in some situations, this could be detrimental to the test takers.

Test choice is sometimes constrained by the time available for testing. This is reflected in a preference for using timed tests rather than untimed tests, and for choosing short tests rather than long tests. There are, unfortunately, examples of tests that are designed to be given untimed being administered with time limits. Obviously, this means that some test takers would have obtained higher scores if they had been given more time to take the test.

Short tests are generally less reliable than longer tests. This means that there is more measurement error associated with the test scores. If scores were reported as a probable score range rather than as single test scores, this would be readily apparent. In practice, short tests may be suitable for scientific purposes or in evaluation studies where the focus is on scores from groups of respondents, but they are of less use when decisions are being made about individuals.

The decision about whether to use timed tests is more complex. It raises issues such as whether working quickly is important in the task whose performance is being predicted. Some theorists argue that speed of response is an essential component of ability testing. However, the time limits for most tests do not put an undue emphasis on speed of response and, typically, they are based on the assumption that about three-quarters of the test takers will be able to complete the test in the time allowed.

In some tests, however, speed of performance is an essential component. Tests of clerical accuracy, for instance, which typically involve checking for errors, are usually highly speeded because it is not the ability to detect errors that is of interest. The errors in individual items are easy to spot, but it is the number of errors that an individual can detect in a given time limit that is of interest. Such tests are more susceptible to practice effects than other tests.

Administering the test

Faulty administration is another common error in test use. The administration of many occupational tests is frequently delegated by the test user to a test administrator. Although this person should be trained, they need not be a qualified user of the test. This might lead to some confusion as to who is really responsible for the test session and it is important that test users are clear that *they* are responsible for such test sessions.

We have already noted that one of the key elements in the definition of testing is that testing is a standardized procedure. How the test is actually administered is a crucial element of this. Most test manuals contain precise instructions as to how the test should be administered. This includes the exact wording that the person administering the test should use.

Test manuals will also usually specify as part of their general instructions how any practice items should be dealt with. Timed tests, in particular, require that the instructions for the start and finish of the test are strictly adhered to. Some test manuals will also instruct the test administrator to tell test takers when they have had half the allotted time, or when they have five minutes left. As most tests are interpreted by comparing the scores of individuals who have taken the test in a single test session with the scores of a reference group who have taken the test at another time but under identical conditions (in so far as this is possible), any departure from the precise instructions for the test's administration will introduce some unknown error into the testing process.

Another important responsibility of anyone administering tests is to keep a log of the test session. This should include personal details of test takers, the tests used and, at the end of the test session, notes of any problems or departures from normal practice that might have affected the test takers' performance.

During the test session it is the responsibility of the test administrator to check, for example, that the test takers are filling in the answer sheet correctly. At the end of the test session answer sheets should also be checked for ambiguous marking that might cause problems when the test is scored.

Scoring tests

Once tests have been taken they need to be scored before they can be interpreted. Nowadays nearly all tests are capable of being scored by computer, although many are still available with hand-scoring keys. Scoring is really a two-stage process that first involves scoring the test and then converting the raw test scores to norm scores. (See Chapter 5.)

Apart from tests that are administered on computer, most other tests either have reusable question booklets with separate answer sheets or question booklets in which answers are recorded directly. Most publishers offer scoring services for their tests, in which case completed test booklets or answer sheets can be sent to them for scoring (for a fee). The scoring of some tests is so complex that they can only be scored by computer (for example, the Strong Interest Inventory).

Clearly, if scoring services are available the test user will have to specify which norm tables are to be used for scoring. The choice of available norms should be clearly stated by the supplier of the scoring service. Most users have to rely on existing norms, but large-scale users should set about building up their own norm tables which can be used as a replacement for, or in addition to, externally available norms. (See Appendix Figure 1 for instructions on how to calculate percentiles.)

Test users who are using tests to select people for jobs are likely to be using group ability tests or tests of special abilities. If the number of test takers is small, these tests are frequently scored by hand using scoring keys supplied by the test publishers. Scoring of a large number of tests is nearly always carried out by computer and most personality measures are scored by computer, both because of the number of scales they contain and because test users wish to have access to the computer-generated interpretative reports that are available.

Scoring tests by hand is really a simple clerical task and is frequently delegated by the test user. However, it is important that it is done accurately and test users need to ensure that they have appropriate quality control procedures to detect any errors, such as double scoring a subset of answer sheets. For most tests, the raw scores are converted to norm scores by reference to tables supplied in the test manual by the test publisher and test interpretation is based on the norm scores. For American tests or tests developed in other countries, UK test users are likely to want to know whether supplementary British norm tables are available. Such information is usually contained in the test publishers' catalogues.

However, some tests are designed to be interpreted directly on the basis of their raw scores. These include tests designed to look at **intra-individual** differences, for example an individual's preference order for different work activities that use an ipsative item format. Most tests are designed to make comparisons across individuals; these are referred to as **inter-individual** differences.

If scoring is being carried out by computer, or by a test publisher's scoring service, the test user still needs to have procedures to check that scoring has been carried out appropriately. This might include having some answer sheets scored twice and should at least mean that the test user is aware of the quality control procedures that the test publisher applies to their scoring service.

If test scoring and interpretation is being provided by a third party, then the test user, who has the ultimate responsibility for all aspects of the testing process, would also want to know who is taking professional responsibility for the scoring and interpretation service.

Interpreting test scores

Once the test has been scored, the most important part of the whole testing process is interpreting what those scores mean. Most test interpretation is norm-referenced, that is, it is done by comparing the score of one individual on a test with scores on the same test from large representative samples.

The technical issues involved in understanding test scores and the different conventions used by psychologists for reporting test scores were set out in Chapter 5. At this stage we want to emphasize four issues concerned with score interpretation and to note that failure to take into account the limitations of test scores is one of the major weaknesses of much test interpretation. The issues are:

• allowing for measurement error

• using appropriate norms

• providing an interpretation that is sensitive to context

• considering interpretation as prediction.

Allowing for measurement error

Having some understanding of the probable degree of accuracy of test scores is vital to good interpretation. Now that most test scoring is no longer done by hand, there is little excuse for not reporting test scores in terms of confidence limits, that is, the probability that someone's score is within a certain range of the score they obtained on the test.

Once we start to base test interpretations on score ranges rather than on single test scores it becomes much clearer that, just because one person's score, or one test score, is higher than another, it does not necessarily mean that one individual possesses more of the characteristic measured by the test than another, or that one person's standing on one test is better than their relative standing on another test. This is true whether we are comparing the performance of an individual across several different tests (or subtests), or comparing the performance of a number of individuals on the same test. This approach encourages us to think of the degree of confidence with which we can make assertions, and to recognize that all measurement has error associated with it.

One test battery that adopts this approach to reporting test scores is the Differential Aptitude Tests (DAT). An example profile was shown in Figure 5.5.

Using appropriate norms

Some tests have been standardized on large nationally representative samples, while others have been standardized on a variety of different samples, for example, secondary school students, university graduates, or specific occupational groups. For some tests a large number of tables of norms will be available, while for others the number of alternative norm groups is quite small. Samples used in norms groups will also vary in size. They may vary from samples of thousands of people to samples containing no more than a hundred people.

Depending on which norm table is used, an individual's relative standing will vary. A test score that puts an individual in the top ten per cent of the adult population may put them only in the top third of university graduates. If we are making interpretations at the individual level, then it is important that the norm group that is chosen is appropriate for the decision for which the test is being used. It will probably be inappropriate in most situations, for example, to evaluate the performance on an ability test of someone who left school at 16 with norms for university students. However, it might be appropriate if that person was applying for entry to university as a mature student.

When we are evaluating the performance of a group of individuals who have taken the same test, as when we use the test as one stage or component of a selection process, then, while the overall standing of the group will vary depending on the norm table used, their relative standing one to another will not change. However, if the norms used are inappropriate it is possible that variability in the group's test performance might be obscured if they fall at one end or the other of the distribution of scores for that norm group. It may sometimes be easier to work with raw scores from the test in this situation.

Providing an interpretation that is sensitive to context

When a person's test results are compared with a norm group, no real consideration is being given to the particular circumstances or situation in which the test was taken by that individual. It is always possible that for one of a variety of reasons the individual's test performance was unrepresentative of their normal behaviour, or was significantly different from the level of performance that might have been expected from them.

While it may not be possible to get any feedback on these issues until the test results are communicated to the test taker, if testing was conducted properly some information about the test taker should be available before the interpretation of the test results is completed. When test results are interpreted using computer programs the outcomes, typically narrative reports, do not normally take into account anything other than a limited amount of demographic or background information about the test takers, such as their age, sex and occupation, which may be used to identify appropriate norm groups. The test interpretations provided by such reports, therefore, need to be evaluated against the additional information that should be available to the test user before they are communicated to the test takers or used in any decision-making process.

The availability of supporting evidence gives additional confidence to the interpretation of test results. However, such evidence should not be used uncritically. Its reliability and validity needs to be assessed before its worth can be fully evaluated.

Considering interpretation as prediction

In some circumstances the interpretation of test performance is quite direct. For example, a test of educational attainment might be used to identify topics or subject areas where a child needs additional teaching. This could be based almost directly on the child's replies to particular items on the test. In other circumstances, scores on a test of general mental ability might be used to predict future job performance, and therefore to make the decision whether or not to offer a job to the test taker.

Both levels of interpretation rest on assumptions. In the former case they are of a fairly short-range nature and relate to the representativeness and appropriateness of the test. In the latter case the assumptions are more complex and their validation may require considerable evidence.

Tests are used to make a variety of types of decisions. Making decisions on the basis of test scores implies that accurate predictions can be made. However, it is important to remember that most of these predictions are only of a probabilistic nature. They also rest on assumptions that future behaviour can be predicted to a significant extent from present behaviour. This is true in many situations, but not all. Some aspects of human behaviour are prone to day-to-day variation and psychologists distinguish **states**, such as anxiety level, which may vary considerably from day to day from **traits** which are seen more as underlying and stable aspects of the individual.

Similarly, test interpretations vary considerably both in the extent to which they try to predict the future and in the range of concepts that they draw upon. In practice, test interpretations fail if they go beyond the data in the range of predictions that they are used to make and, conversely, may also fail if they do no more than provide a description of the person, because others will put their own interpretations, that is, make their own predictions from that description.

Communicating test findings

Test findings always have to be communicated. Best practice is that the test takers should always get some feedback on their test performance and, in addition, those making decisions on the basis of test results need to have them interpreted.

A major practical concern with the use of tests with children and young people is who should have access to the results of testing. Should results always be presented to the child or young person, should their parents have a right to see the test results, or is it reasonable that the school or educational institution alone should have access to the test results? In the past the results from much educational testing and assessment were not communicated to the test takers (children and young people) or their parents. Increasingly, this practice is being questioned and current standards of good practice suggest that test takers should expect to have their test results explained to them. One argument frequently used by those who suggest that test results need not, or should not, necessarily be communicated to test takers is that it is very difficult to present test data in a way that children, young people and their parents can understand. This argument always seems to me to be something of a smoke screen. It may stem from élitism, implying that the test takers would not understand their own test results, or it may conceal the fact that the person with access to the test results is not confident that they can explain or fully interpret the test results to the test taker. No doubt providing a clear interpretation of test results in a non-technical and jargon-free manner will result in extra work, but there is no doubt that it can be done and, by doing so, much of the fear and suspicion of testing is likely to be dissipated.

Communicating to the test taker

The communication of test results to the test taker, in many circumstances, can be considered as a second stage in the process of test interpretation. Frequently, it is only when the results are communicated that some issues about the context in which testing took place can be discussed. One part of this process is, therefore, concerned with getting reactions from the test takers to the process of testing, that is finding out whether there were any special circumstances that might have affected their test performance and their reactions to the tests in general terms. For example, if the tests included measures of maximum performance, the test takers' perceptions of the difficulty of the test, or about particular types of question, numerical items for instance, help to provide a context for understanding their test performance.

Test results must always be evaluated in the context of other information that might be available about the test taker. If the test results appear congruent with this information, this can be considered as validating the test findings – two sources of information are generally regarded as better than one. If test results are discrepant with other information about the test taker, or if the test taker feels the test results are not representative of their normal performance, this must be recognized. However reliable a test is in general, and even if the standard error of test scores has been reported, there is always a probability that the test score, or score range, suggested by the test for a particular test taker is subject to significant error, that is, error greater than that which would normally be expected by chance. Testing is not a perfectly objective process. In these circumstance there is only limited value in trying to decide which source of information should be believed. It is almost certainly going to be more useful to discuss constructively with the test taker how they would like to proceed. Should the results of testing be ignored? Should additional information be sought? If so, should that be from another test, from taking the same test again, or seeking out other sources of information, for example teachers or educational records in addition to those that may have already been consulted?

The extent to which it is sensible to question test results will also be influenced by the data available on the reliability of the test. Many measures of typical performance are less reliable than measures of maximum performance and, as we have already noted (see Chapter 3), the acceptance of some test results can be influenced by the 'Barnum effect'.

There are a number of more general points that need to be borne in mind when presenting test results to test takers. First of all, it is important that the results are not obscured by jargon or technical terms. As we have already stressed, the presentation of test results needs to take into account what is already known about the test taker, and the positive aspects of the test results should be stressed. When the test taker is also the test user, a primary purpose of testing will have been to empower the test taker. This implies that testing is used to raise self-esteem and promote self-awareness, and not the opposite. Even when test results are not being used in this way, but are just being reported to the test taker, the communication process should aim to be constructive and to leave the test taker feeling that testing has benefited them.

Ideally, test results should be communicated to the test taker in person. It would be very unusual for this not be the case when the test taker is also the test user, for example in career counselling. However, in some situations it is possible that test takers will receive only written feedback on their test performance. This might be where applicants have taken tests as part of the selection process for a job or in large-scale screening programmes, such as the routine testing of all schoolchildren in a particular locality.

Figure 7.3 summarizes key points to bear in mind when providing feedback on test results. Many tests provide a written version of the test results for the test taker to take away. These often provide background information on the test and its interpretation.

The difficulty of providing feedback to test takers who have failed to get a job, possibly as a result of their test scores, should not be underestimated. Many organizations do not give feedback for this reason, although best professional practice is that test takers should always be given feedback on their test performance. Particular difficulties, in such situations, are that test users often feel they will have to justify their decision not to offer a job. In addition, they sometimes feel they would have to provide careers advice or feedback on other parts of the selection process as well. In such circumstances the best option might be to provide written feedback that concentrates on the test performance alone. The written feedback should make clear how the test scores were used and provide appropriate normative information to enable the test takers to understand their own scores. There should always be a contact name for test takers to consult if they need more information or help in understanding their test scores.

Another situation where written feedback may be all that can be provided is where tests are administered as part of a screening programme. In Britain it is rare for children or their parents to be offered feedback from much of the educational testing that is routinely carried out by schools. It appears that such testing is carried out exclusively for the school's or education system's benefit and that the rights of test takers are ignored. However, it would be relatively straightforward to provide written feedback in these cases, which usually involve ability or attainment tests for which local or national norms are likely to be available. Figure 7.4 provides an example of what such a report might look like. As well as giving the child's test scores, it gives some information about how to interpret the scores, describes how they will be used, gives a short description of what the test involved and a contact point from which further information can be obtained.

A particular concern when tests are administered in this way is that the results may be entered on educational records without having been prop-

---

Figure 7.3 Key points on providing test feedback

1. Evaluate test results in conjunction with other information that is available about the test taker.
2. Be sensitive to the context in which testing has taken place.
3. Do not overinterpret a single test score.
4. Remember that test scores for individuals are less reliable than test scores for groups.
5. Seek the reaction of the test taker to the test results.
6. Present test results in non-technical language.
7. Remember that receiving test results is often stressful for the test taker.
8. Offer the opportunity for the test takers to talk further about this test results.
9. Present test results in a constructive way, so that the test takers feel they have benefited from testing.

---

erly interpreted. Decisions may be made on the basis of the test results without any special circumstances that may have affected an individual's performance being recorded, and without reference to any background information that might be relevant. Essentially, no check is being made on the context in which testing took place and this, inevitably, lowers the quality of the testing process and of any decisions made on the basis of those results.

One issue that may arise when test results are being communicated to the test takers or their representative (e.g. parents of young children) is that the people responsible for writing or giving feedback may soften their interpretation to avoid causing unnecessary distress. This may be appropriate, but the quality of the testing process is also undermined if it results in loss of precision in test interpretation. It may also make any recommendations that are given on the basis of the test results appear misleading.

Communicating to the decision-maker

When tests have been administered and interpreted by one person who has to communicate the results to another person to use in decision-making, many of the same issues apply as when the results are being communicated to the test taker. The test results will need to be put into context and communicated in a non-technical manner and in such a way that their limitations are properly understood. Clearly, there are different pressures involved if it is the test result of a single individual that is being discussed as opposed to the results from 100 job applicants or 250 schoolchildren.

Figure 7.4 Example written report

Arithmetic Attainment Test
Report for Pupil and Parents or Guardian
For: John Richards   Year: 5   School: Dawson   Date: Spring 1995

Test results

Your child scored **63** out of a possible maximum score of 80. This means that your child answered **79** per cent of the questions correctly.

How to interpret test scores

The test results of your child can be compared with those of other children in Year 5 in the county.

There were 80 questions on the Arithmetic Attainment Test:
1. The middle ranking child in the county achieved a score of 55, that is answered 69 per cent of the questions correctly.
2. Your child's score of **63** on the test was better than **72** per cent of children in this year group in the county.

How confident you can be in the test results

Test performance can vary. Your child might have done slightly better, or worse, on this test on a different occasion. The margin of error associated with scores on this test is plus or minus 3 score points and it is 95 per cent certain that your child's score is in the range **60-66**.

How the test scores will be used

The results of this test will be considered in making educational decisions about your child. Other information including reports from your child's teachers will also considered.

Description of what the test measures

The test measures key arithmetical skills for children at this level. These skills include:

1. Simple arithmetic (e.g. calculations involving addition, subtraction, multiplication and division).
2. Use of multiplication tables.
3. Use of decimals and fractions and handling money (e.g. working out the correct amount of change).
4. Calculations using time (e.g. calculating the length of time a train journey takes from arrival and departure times).

Further information

If you would like further information about this test and how the test results will be used, or the opportunity to discuss your child's test performance, please contact:

The Headteacher, Dawson Primary School

In large-scale testing programmes, the decision-maker may be less interested in the test results of individuals and the only contextual information to consider is that which affects the group as a whole. However, if decisions are being made about individuals, either as a result of the testing that they have participated in as part of a large group, or on their own, the availability of information about the individual would improve the quality of testing outcomes. In so far as it is only rarely possible to incorporate this kind of information, the quality of the decisions made is lowered.

It is, of course, slightly different if testing is being carried out for screening purposes, because the follow-up to screening will provide the opportunity to collect the additional contextual information.

As we have already outlined, detailed information on the individual being tested, and of the context of testing, is probably only going to be available if the test results have already been communicated to the test taker. However, test results will often have been communicated to the decision-maker and decisions made before the test taker is informed of the test results. Although this may be an inevitable consequence of organizational decision-making practice, it is not ideal when considered purely from the perspective of achieving the best possible decision. It may be that in many cases the cost of changing the sequence, that is the practical difficulties involved, would outweigh the benefits in terms of improved decision-making.

For how long are test scores useful?

Once a test has been taken, scored, interpreted and the results communicated, for how long should those test results be used? What is the 'shelf life' of test scores? There is no doubt that the usefulness of test scores for decision-making decreases over time. This is shown by the test-retest reliability data that are reported in most test manuals. The longer the interval between testing, the lower the correlation between the first set of test scores and the second. When the reliability of a test is measured in this way, what is really being evaluated is the stability of what the test measures. This will vary because of test content and because of changes within individuals and/or their situation. On most tests, scores for children change more rapidly than scores for adults.

As a rule of thumb, the 'shelf life' of test results should be no more than one year. By this, I mean that test results more than 12 months old should no longer be used for making decisions about an individual. For children and young people, or where there are other reasons to think that a person's test performance might have changed considerably, even six months might be too long. Educational testing is particularly prone to changes if individuals have not been properly prepared for assessment, or have been deprived of the relevant educational experiences and then receive more appropriate education or training.

Clearly, the decision whether to take a test again is a complex one. Where tests are being used for counselling or careers advice, the decision will be taken by the client who is both the test taker and test user. In other situations, such as the use of tests for selection, the rights of the test takers are being safeguarded by giving them the opportunity to be reassessed.

When tests are used as a routine part of a selection procedure, some organizations specify minimum times that must elapse before tests can be retaken. This is to stop people reapplying to take the test again immediately. The British Civil Service requires applicants without relevant educational qualifications to sit a selection test for administrative assistant posts. If they are turned down, applicants normally have to wait six months before they can reapply.

Limitations to testing

It is important to remember that testing has limitations. While there are advantages that should flow from the proper use of tests, tests are not designed to provide, and are not capable of providing, certain kinds of information. Tyler (1984) listed the following limitations of testing:

- Tests cannot measure unique characteristics; they measure only traits common to many people.

- Tests provide little information on development or dynamics.

- Tests do not provide information on background or context.

- Intelligence, personality, abilities and interests are not static; tests do not provide information on whether and how these might change over time.

These limitations are inherent in tests. In the preceding sections of this chapter we have raised many issues that affect proper test use. These serve to remind us that it is the way in which tests are used that is far more important than the quality of particular tests themselves. While lack of information about a test may limit its usefulness, lack of understanding of how to use tests properly, particularly how to interpret test scores and how to communicate test results meaningfully, is a far more significant threat to testing. Misuse of tests not only affects the particular situation in which a test was being used but, as far as the general public is concerned, tends to undermine the credibility of all test use.

Summary

This chapter has set out to review the issues that make for the proper use of tests. It has covered all stages of the testing process. Key stages include:

- being clear why tests are being used

- making sure that test takers are advised how to prepare to take tests

- choosing tests that are appropriate for the decision being made and to the people being tested

- being aware that inappropriate test choice is one of the most common areas of test misuse

- using correct procedures to administer the test

- making sure that scoring is carried out properly

- interpreting test scores in a way that recognizes measurement error and uses appropriate norms to provide an interpretation that is sensitive to the context of testing

- considering test interpretation as prediction but being aware of the assumptions made when test results are used in this way

- communicating test findings to the test taker in an appropriate manner

- communicating test results to any decision-maker in a way that will inform the decision-making process

- recognizing that test scores have a limited useful life.

Finally, it should always be recognized that there are limitations to testing. Tests are not designed to provide, and are not capable of providing, certain kinds of information.

8 How to find out about tests

Finding out about tests is not straightforward. In the last ten years or so, considerable changes have taken place in Britain in the way tests are distributed and in how training in test use is organized and accredited. In this chapter we start by reviewing the changes that have taken place in test publishing and in training and accreditation as they have important consequences for anyone who wants to find out about psychological tests.

The recent changes – test publishing

In recent years, as new publishers and distributors have set up to take advantage of the increased demand for psychological tests, the world of test publishing has become increasingly fragmented. The growing market for tests for use in recruitment and selection, and the increase in the number of psychologists working in this area, have both contributed to making more complex the whole process of finding out about tests. In the past, the number of test publishers was small and nearly all the major US test publishers used the same UK distributor. This is no longer the case. Different US publishers now have links with various UK publishers and at least one US test publisher has set up its own UK office. A significant number of new UK publishers have also been established, making the market place for psychological tests more complex than ever before. This is the first major stumbling block for anyone wanting to find out about tests: the number of places from which you can purchase tests has increased considerably.

Secondly, it is important to realize that test publishers are not like supermarkets, where the same manufacturers' goods are available (but possibly at different prices). You cannot just visit one and browse through the goods before deciding what to purchase. Tests are effectively bought direct from the manufacturer. Each test publisher sells a unique range of tests, so that to find out about the main personality questionnaires on the market it would be necessary to obtain the catalogues from several different test publishers.

Thirdly, test supply is a mail order business, so shopping is by post. This means that a range of goods cannot be inspected before they are purchased.

Finally, publishers will not sell their products to you unless they think you are qualified to use them. The mechanics of this process are described in more detail in Chapter 9. However, the important point to note is that potential purchasers of psychological tests have to become qualified test users before they can buy tests.

The recent changes – training and accreditation

The changes taking place in test publishing alongside the increased use of psychological tests in the occupational area has led to professional organizations, such as The British Psychological Society (BPS) and the Institute of Personnel and Development (IPD), becoming increasingly aware of their role in promoting best practice in testing. The leading test publishers have also recognized this concern.

The basis of the current approach to training and accreditation is that publishers will not sell tests to people not considered qualified to use them. Potential purchasers of tests have to register with the test publishers, who will want to know whether individuals are qualified to use particular tests.

In the past The British Psychological Society used to accredit training courses in psychological testing. Specific training courses would qualify individuals to use certain types of tests. Tests were broadly grouped into certain well-defined categories – group tests of ability; interest inventories; personality measures. There were also some training courses that focused on specific tests. The purchase of many tests was restricted to psychologists who could demonstrate that they had the necessary expertise to use them.

However, the system was imperfect in a number of respects. By regulating courses and not the competences of individuals who had received training, it was essentially controlling the input to training and not the output from training. Psychologists who were members of one of the professional divisions of The British Psychological Society were allowed to purchase any test. It was assumed that they would not purchase or use a test that they were not competent to use.

The changes in training and accreditation affect both psychologists and non-psychologists. The intention is to move to a situation where the only distinction made is between people who can provide evidence of their competence to use tests and those who cannot provide such evidence.

Registration of Psychologists

Since 1988, The British Psychological Society has maintained a Register of Chartered Psychologists. To join the register a psychologist must have obtained an accredited first degree in psychology (or equivalent qualification) and also have completed at least three years' further study or practice in psychology at a level that is judged sufficient for the individual to practise professionally without supervision.

Although there is no legal requirement for psychologists to join the register, only those members of the BPS who are on the register can call themselves Chartered Psychologists. Chartered Psychologists agree to abide by a code of conduct that includes the requirement that they do not claim competence that they do not possess. As far as psychological testing is concerned, this means not using any test that the Chartered Psychologist is not competent to use. Although this implies that Chartered Psychologists will regulate themselves, the BPS has a disciplinary committee that investigates complaints of professional malpractice and which can, and does, remove individuals from the register.

The competence approach

The move to a competence approach to training and accreditation of test users has been gradual and is still in process. The full details of the scheme, and how it affects individuals who want to become qualified test users, are described in Chapter 9. The process is run by the BPS which issues Certificates of Competence that are recognized by the major test publishers as evidence that someone is competent to use tests at a particular level.

The Level A Certificate of Competence in Occupational Testing was introduced in 1991. This covers most group tests of ability, interest inventories and a range of careers guidance materials. The Level B Certificate of Competence, which has been introduced more recently, covers personality assessment and is structured in two stages. The Intermediate Level B Certificate of Competence is a foundation qualification for people qualified to use a single personality measure, and the Full Level B Certificate is awarded to those who have demonstrated their competence to use a number of personality measures and have also acquired skills in test choice and evaluation.

This approach has been endorsed by the IPD and the major test publishers. So far about 6,000 people have been awarded the Level A Certificate of Competence and a further 3,000 have been awarded the Level A Statement of Competence, indicating that they were already qualified under previous procedures to use tests at this level. Approximately 1,500 new Level A Certificates of Competence in Occupational Testing are issued each year.

While the number of people who might be expected to obtain the Level B qualification will be smaller than this, the new proposals have widespread support. Once the Level B Certificate is established, the vast majority of non-psychologists who wish to use tests will have a clear route to becoming qualified users of a wide range of tests that will meet most, if not all, of their requirements.

The BPS Steering Committee on Test Standards is also exploring the applicability of the competence-based approach to more specialized areas of assessment in educational and clinical psychology. Most, but not all, use of psychological tests in these areas is performed by psychologists, and frequently involves the use of tests designed for individual assessment. Many of these tests require specific training, as their use may involve apparatus, timing of responses and making judgements about how to score the verbal responses of the test taker.

Bartram (1995) sees the main advantage of the new scheme as being that it makes standards explicit. He identifies five areas of benefit.

- There is a clear specification of what potential test users need to be able to do and know in order to use tests properly.

- Specific objectives for participants on training courses exist which they can match against the content of the training course.

- Training routes are potentially flexible with the possibility of accrediting work experience and the use of open-learning materials and short courses.

- Transferability of qualification is made possible because the new qualifications make explicit the skills and knowledge that qualified people can be expected to possess.

- The existence of a nationally defined professional standard will have major advantages for employers.

If the new approach to training and accreditation of test users is successful, it should lead to better use of tests. These benefits might be realized in a variety of ways – for example, by improved standards of test administration, and by a more appropriate choice of tests. Improving the quality of psychological testing should result in the quality of decisions made on the basis of psychological testing having greater validity, with consequent benefits to all users of test results. For employers, it means better selection and placement decisions, for example, while individuals will benefit from more accurate assessment, better careers advice and so on.

Sources of information

The main sources of information that need to be consulted to find out about tests are:

• test publishers and their catalogues

• test manuals

• test reviews

• other test users

• expert advice.

Each of these will now be discussed in detail.

Test publishers and their catalogues

Test publishers are, perhaps, the natural starting point for finding out about tests. A test publisher's catalogue describes in some detail the tests they sell. A catalogue should make clear for whom the test is designed, the training required to use the test, whether it is a timed test and, if so, how long it takes to administer, and so on. However, potential test users should be aware that these are marketing tools. For each test, a catalogue will list all the materials that are available. An example list of the materials that might be available for a single test is shown in Figure 8.1.

There are several points to note about such a list. Many tests are available in more than one version. These might be alternate forms that are designed to be equivalent, or versions of the test designed for different age or ability groups; the catalogue will describe the different versions in more detail. For some tests, there may be four or five different versions available. Most tests are supplied with reusable question booklets and separate answer sheets. The same answer sheets might be capable of being used with both versions of the test, or there might be different answer sheets for different versions.

Many tests can be hand scored and to do this most will have scoring keys, usually stencils, that can be laid over the answer sheet. For a test of maximum performance, such as an ability test, this will identify the

---

Figure 8.1 Test catalogue entry (hypothetical example)

1. Test booklets – Form A – reusable (25)
2. Test booklets – Form B – reusable (25)
3. Answer sheets – pack of 50
4. Scoring Keys – Form A
5. Scoring Keys – Form B
6. Manual
7. Supplement of UK norms
8. Specimen set

Each item on the list would be separately priced.

---

correct answers, so that scores can be added up. For tests of typical performance, such as interest inventories and personality measures, there may be one scoring key for each scale on the test. The key will identify answers and sometimes apply a weighting to them. For example if there are three alternative answers to a test item – (a) frequently, (b) sometimes, (c) never – answer (a) might be scored 2 and answer (b) 1 on the scale.

Many publishers now offer scoring services, where answer sheets are sent to the publisher for scoring and interpretation. For some tests, particularly measures of personality, the publisher might offer a variety of levels of scoring. These can range from providing a score profile against standard norms to computer-generated narrative reports. Some tests can only be computer-scored.

Computer-administered tests will be scored automatically by the computer program that administers the test. Some level of interpretation using norms held on the computer may also be provided. The test user would have to specify which norms are to be used for scoring the answers of a particular test taker.

Most tests are available as specimen sets. A **specimen set** would normally include one set of all the test material, that is it would contain a test manual, question booklet, answer sheet, scoring key, and so on. It is designed to allow a potential user to evaluate the test, supplying all the material that would be required to use it.

In addition to producing catalogues, most test publishers also employ psychologists who can answer questions that the potential purchaser might want to ask about a particular test. Test publishers will not sell tests to people unless they think they are qualified to use them. The procedures for becoming qualified to use tests in the UK are described in detail in Chapter 9. However, it is worth pointing out that most test publishers provide test training as well as selling tests.

Test manuals

The test manual is the key reference document for the test. It describes in detail how the test should be used, its design and development, administration and scoring procedures. It will contain tables of norms, describe how the test was standardized, and cite evidence for the reliability and validity of the test for the purposes for which it was designed. Figure 8.2 details the information that a potential test user should expect to be available in a test manual. In practice, the quality of test manuals varies considerably. They are usually revised relatively infrequently. Consequently, when used alone they are not always as complete a source of information about a test as might be desired.

While test manuals will be updated periodically, for many tests supplementary handbooks or additional tables of norms are produced separately by the publisher. If a test was designed and developed in the USA, it is possible that the UK publisher will have produced a supplement of UK norms. Frequently, these are only relatively small-scale studies and the representativeness of some norm groups needs to be questioned. However, some of the most widely used personality measures, for example the Sixteen Personality Factor (16PF) questionnaire distributed by ASE, and the Occupational Personality Questionnaire (OPQ) published by Saville and Holdsworth, have been standardized on representative samples of the UK population. Currently, Oxford Psychologists Press is about to launch a study to standardize three tests that it distributes in the UK. These are the California Psychological Inventory (CPI), Myers-Briggs Type Indicator (MBTI), and the FIRO-B, a measure of interpersonal behaviour.

Test reviews

Test reviews are another major source of information that the potential test purchaser will need to consult. For many years, Oscar Buros' *Mental Measurements Yearbooks* (MMY) were the main source of test reviews (see Chapter 2). *The Twelfth Mental Measurements Yearbook* was published in 1995 (Conoley and Impara) and reviews tests that were published or revised since the publication of the Eleventh *MMY* in 1992 (Kramer and Conoley). A supplement to the Eleventh *MMY* was published in 1994 (Conoley and Impara). As well as including test reviews (sometimes more than one) for each test, it also includes a bibliography for the test that lists articles and reviews published elsewhere. The Tenth, Eleventh and Twelfth *MMY*s and the semi-annual update volumes are in the process of being made available for computerized search.

Figure 8.2   Information required in a test manual

1. **Purpose:** The introduction should set out the main purposes for which the test should be used and other key features of the test, such as the existence of versions for different target populations or situations.

2. **Background information:** This section should contain information on the development and design of the test. It should cite references to research that was conducted as part of the development process.

3. **Test administration:** Detailed instructions about how the test should be administered should be set out. These normally include precise wordings that the test administrator should use. If there are practice items for the test, how to administer and score these items should be described, including how to explain the answers to practice items to candidates. Instructions on the time required for test administration and examples of replies to questions that candidates might ask should also be specified.

4. **Scoring procedures:** Arrangements for scoring should be described. How to use scoring keys, when appropriate, should also be explained. Appropriate checks that should be carried out as part of the scoring process and how to total raw scores should also be covered. If a scoring service is being used, procedures for using the service should be described as well as any checks that should be made on the answer sheets or question booklets before they are sent for scoring.

5. **Standardization:** Details of how the test was standardized should be described. These should include details of sample sizes, description of the sample and how it was chosen, so that its representativeness can be evaluated.

6. **Norm tables:** How raw test scores are converted to norm scores (percentiles or standard scores) should be explained. Guidance should be given on selecting from the various norm tables that are provided. Standard error of measurement for scores should be specified and appropriate confidence intervals for test scores specified.

7. **Reliability:** The procedures that have been used to assess the reliability of the test should be described. These might include measures of the internal consistency of scales or the test, measures of equivalence between alternate forms of the same test (correlations obtained when different versions of the same test have been administered to the same people), measures of the stability of test scores over different time periods (correlations between test scores obtained at time 1 with those obtained at time 2). Information should be available for all scales included in the test, as they will not necessarily be equally reliable, and from samples that differ on key dimensions (e.g. age).

8. **Validity:** Evidence should be given about the appropriateness of the test for its intended purpose. This normally covers the three facets of validity: content, construct and criterion-related validity. This might include evidence that the test makes accurate predictions or diagnoses, positive correlations between the test and other tests designed to measure similar attributes (convergent validity) and low correlations with tests designed to measure different attributes (divergent validity). When evidence from concurrent validity studies is being used as a substitute for predictive validation, this should be noted. Descriptions of key studies carried out as part of test development should also be included and references given to other studies that describe the use of the test.

9. **Fairness:** Studies undertaken to examine item bias should be described. It should be explained why using the test with certain types of people may be inappropriate. Known limitations should be described.

10. **Interpretation:** How to interpret the test results should be explained with examples. Key points that need to be communicated about the reliability and validity of test scores should be mentioned. Written reports and profile sheets used for presenting test results to test takers should be described.

The *Mental Measurements Yearbooks* are the standard reference works that provide detailed, but frequently technical, reviews of tests. The reviews are designed to be read by qualified and, some might say, expert test users. The novice test user might be rather overwhelmed by them. Another difficulty in relying on the *MMY* as a source of information is that it is a US publication and may ignore some British tests that are widely used in the UK but hardly used at all in the USA. In the past its intermittent publication meant that it was unlikely to contain reviews of recently published tests, but now that it has adopted a three-year publication cycle this is less likely to be the case. Over its fifty-plus year history, the *MMY* and its associated publications have established themselves as the standard reference books on tests.

Until recently there was no equivalent reference source available in the UK. However, aware of the value of test reviews, the BPS Steering Committee on Test Standards and BPS Books have published two compendiums of specially commissioned test reviews. The first of these publications, *A Review of Psychometric Tests for Assessment in Vocational Training* (Bartram *et al.*, 1990) was produced originally by the Training Agency but republished with an update by the BPS in 1992. The BPS has now also published the *Review of Personality Assessment Instruments (Level B) for use in Occupational Settings* (Bartram *et al.*, 1995).

The original *Review* (Bartram *et al.*, 1990) covered 59 tests. In the introduction, it noted that 'the quality of the tests and of their documentation varied enormously'. The original volume covered a range of commonly used ability and aptitude tests and interest inventories. These are tests that someone holding the Level A Certificate (or Statement) of Competence in Occupational Testing would normally be qualified to use.

The information covered in each individual test review is shown in Figure 8.3. The reviews were structured under five broad headings: test details, general information, administration and scoring, documentation, and evaluation.

The book raised a number of general points about the tests it reviewed. In particular it reported that, in terms of overall technical quality, 14 of the 59 tests were classified as 'less than adequate', 15 as 'adequate', 24 as 'reasonable' and only 6 as 'good'. As far as validity data were concerned, 28 tests were rated as 'less than adequate', 13 as 'adequate', 16 as 'reasonable' and only 2 as 'good'. No tests were rated as excellent on either technical quality or validity.

The *Review of Personality Assessment Instruments (Level B) for use in Occupational Settings* (Bartram *et al.*, 1995) provides reviews of 30 personality measures. The test reviews present information in the same structure and format as the earlier set.

Figure 8.3   Information in test reviews

1. **Test Details** – This covers the following areas:
   a) Basic information about the test: title, publisher, distributor, author(s), date of publication
   b) Type of test
   c) Supply conditions – qualifications required to use test
   d) Age range for which test is applicable
   e) Alternate forms of the test available
   f) Format – paper-and-pencil or computerized
   g) Reference set cost (excluding training costs)
   h) Cost per candidate of test materials.

2. **General Description** – What the test is, its scales, points of special interest, key features. Relevant background information.

3. **Administration and Scoring** – This covers:
   a) Facilities required
   b) Scoring and interpretation services available
   c) Time requirements for preparation, administration, scoring and interpretation.

4. **Documentation** – Ratings of key aspects of documentation contained in the test manual and relevant supplementary material. This includes:
   a) Ratings of technical information under the following main headings: validity, reliability, norm tables
   b) Ratings of clarity and coverage of content under the following main headings: rationale, development, standardization, norms, reliability, validity, administration, scoring, interpretation, feedback to candidates, bias, restrictions on use, references and supporting materials.

5. **Evaluation** – Comments on the ratings given under four headings:
   a) Evaluation of technical information
   b) Design of the test
   c) Overall evaluation – reviewers' judgements about the test
   d) Conclusion – summary and recommendations.

For most people who wish to use tests in the UK, these two volumes provide a valuable source of impartial advice. Consulting them should be an important part of any search for information about tests currently available in the UK.

One difficulty in evaluating reviews is that they are time-dependent. As Buros found, it takes several years to construct a large-scale set of reviews. No sooner are they published than they start to go out of date as tests are revised, new studies using the tests are published, and so on. At the present time, the two BPS Reviews represent an invaluable source of detailed and insightful comment on tests widely used in the UK. However, to maintain their usefulness, the regular updating and revision that is promised will need to be meticulously adhered to.

It should be noted that there are a number of other sources of test reviews. *Test Critiques* is a series of test reviews published by the Test Corporation of America. There are currently six volumes in the series. Reviews of tests also appear in some professional and academic journals. In the occupational area, a relatively new publication is the *Test Validity Yearbook* (Landy, 1992) which reports original validation research rather than judgemental reviews.

While reviews remind any potential test user of the limitations of tests, the test user still has to take final responsibility for choosing which tests to use. A test with some faults may still be useful in many situations. Well-informed and careful use of tests may be better than relying exclusively on other sources of information that may be even harder to evaluate.

However, test users should not forget that the purpose of reviews is to inform their test use and that reviews were originally written because the technical qualities of tests vary considerably.

Other test users

For the inexperienced test user, talking to other more experienced test users can be helpful. This is not without risks, however, because there are many technical issues about which many users may be only partially informed. Nevertheless, other users of a specific test can often give helpful tips on its use. They may also be aware of validation studies or normative data that are available.

In theory, test publishers should act as reference points for the tests they publish. If I was contemplating making a major investment in test materials – if I were setting up a large-scale selection programme, for instance – I would certainly ask the publishers of the test(s) I was considering using to refer me to existing users of the test. I would then discuss with these test users their experience of using them. A complete set of test materials is likely to cost several hundred pounds, so it seems sensible to do some checking first.

Expert advice

In theory, the idea that there ought to be 'experts' in testing from whom it would be possible to get 'good' advice sounds appealing. However, as the market for tests gets larger and more complex, few people can claim to be really expert in more than a small part of it. If one wants detailed information on specific tests, then test reviews and publishers' catalogues are the best sources of advice. Experienced users of particular tests are a valuable source of advice if they can be tracked down. Some tests have user groups associated with them. Their role is discussed in greater detail in Chapter 9 and contact addresses for the British Association for Psychological Type, which is a focus for expertise on the Myers-Briggs Type Indicator, and the 16PF Users Group are given in 'Sources of further information' (page 162).

Chartered Psychologists are one potential source of expertise. The BPS publishes a *Directory of Chartered Psychologists* and the services they offer. However, as people have to pay for entries, it is really a form of 'yellow pages' and not a register of all Chartered Psychologists. The BPS Division of Occupational Psychology has published a yearbook (1994) for its own members that lists their interests and the services that they offer.

In practice, experts have to be found by networking. They are the people who speak at conferences and write articles in professional and academic journals. Real experts 'know what they don't know' but will probably also 'know someone who does'. However, as testing is now a major business activity for many psychologists, advice is not always disinterested.

Professional organizations are also sources of information. The British Psychological Society has a Steering Committee on Test Standards which has just updated its free guide to testing (*Psychological Testing: A User's Guide*, Steering Committee on Test Standards, 1996) and the Institute of Personnel and Development publishes the IPD *Code on Psychological Testing* (undated). Both these documents set out policy and aim to define good practice on testing.

People with only limited experience of using tests need advice if they are to become better and more critical consumers of psychological testing. By being critical consumers they will also raise the standard of products on the market, because poor products will find it harder to compete once their weaknesses become known.

In the past there was the notion of the disinterested professional from whom it was possible to get impartial advice. As testing has become more and more commercial and competitive it seems to be increasingly difficult to get advice that does not come from someone with a vested interest in a particular product. There have even been reports of people being threatened with libel action if they questioned other people's use of tests.

Making an informed choice

Making an informed choice about which test to choose for a particular situation will involve a number of stages. The first stage is being clear about the situation in which you want to use tests. Is it for selecting people for jobs or to give careers advice? What sort of people will you be testing? Both these issues will affect your choice of test and, in the first instance, answering these questions narrows and focuses the search.

The second stage is collecting existing published information about tests. This is likely to include looking at a selection of test publishers' current catalogues, which are usually updated yearly, and examining reviews of any tests you are considering.

Structured reviews, such as those produced by the BPS that were described in the previous section, provide a clear framework for collating information about a range of tests. Consulting the publishers' catalogues will allow you to update the information contained in the reviews. This will alert you to new versions of tests, other supplementary material that might have been published since the review was completed, current costs and so on. Sometimes you will find that a test has changed its publisher since it was reviewed. This might be because the US publisher has changed its UK distributor, or because the test developer, the person who originally developed the test and owns the copyright, has struck a new deal with another test publisher.

At this stage you will probably realize that, if you are not already trained to use the tests you wish to purchase, you need to be. Full details of the current UK system for becoming qualified to use tests are given in the next chapter.

If you are already appropriately qualified to use the tests, the next stage will be to seek out more detailed advice about the tests you are considering using. At this point it would probably be helpful to talk to other people who have used the tests. While it is not always straightforward to identify such people and there is no guarantee that they will be willing to talk to you, I believe that there is real value in talking to someone who has used the test in a similar setting. This is particularly so if the decision is about whether to install a large-scale testing programme, where an organization might want to be clear about the economic and other benefits of testing. If other test users can be identified, they may well be willing to share their experiences of using a test.

At the same time it may be a good idea to purchase specimen sets for the one or two tests that appear most suitable. This will allow you to evaluate the test materials first hand and to compare your impressions with reviewers' comments. It will also allow you to see whether norm data are available for populations of test takers similar to your target group.

Summary

This chapter has aimed to help the potential test user through the maze of information that exists about tests. We started out by examining the recent changes that have taken place in test publishing, and training and accreditation procedures. The process of becoming a qualified test user is described in detail in the next chapter.

The second half of the chapter discussed the main sources of information that are available and how you would go about using them if you wanted to find out about particular tests. The main sources of information are:

- test publishers and their catalogues

- test manuals

- test reviews

- other test users

- people who can give expert advice.

Making an informed choice about the test to use involves being clear about the purpose for which the test will be used and making sure that the test is appropriate for the people who will be taking it.

9 Becoming a test user

It should be clear by now that to use any psychological test requires training. For reasons outlined in the previous chapter, The British Psychological Society (BPS) and the major test publishers in the UK have recently adopted a new approach to the certification of people qualified to use tests. The scheme has been introduced to meet the considerable concern felt by test publishers, experts in psychological testing who were members of the BPS Steering Committee on Test Standards, psychologists and personnel specialists about the way tests were being used. Although the focus of this concern was the way tests were being used in occupational settings, primarily for personnel selection, there was also a need to improve test use in all areas. This included the use of tests by psychologists as well as by non-psychologists.

The thrust of the new approach is to certify competence. At the time of writing, the Level A Certificate covers occupational testing, that is, what is required to use most group ability tests and a range of careers guidance instruments. The BPS has set out its proposals for standards for personality assessment (Level B), and these are in the process of being implemented. Information packs describing the Level A and Level B schemes are available free of charge from The British Psychological Society. The Level A and Level B schemes are described in more detail below.

Level A: Occupational testing

The BPS Steering Committee on Test Standards, in conjunction with the major test publishers, has set out seven broad areas of test competence (see Figure 9.1) and, within each area, provides a checklist of particular competences (see Figure 9.2). The Certificate of Competence in Occupational Testing (Level A) was introduced in 1991. It is the only qualification available to people who wish to become trained in the use of occupational tests and is accepted by all the major test publishers. The essence of the

Figure 9.1 Level A: Units of Competence

The seven units of competence are:

1. psychological testing: defining assessment needs (including types of test and underlying theory)
2. the basic principles of scaling and standardization
3. the importance of reliability and validity
4. deciding when psychological tests should or should not be used as part of an assessment process
5. administering tests to one or more candidates and dealing with scoring procedures
6. making appropriate use of test results and providing accurate written and oral feedback to clients and candidates
7. maintaining security and confidentiality of the test materials and the test data.

competence-based approach is that it is the outcome of training, and not merely attendance at a course, that should be assessed.

Assessments of competence must be carried out by Chartered Psychologists who both:

• hold the BPS Certificate in Occupational Testing (Level A), or the equivalent BPS Statement of Competence (The Statement is for those who were already qualified to use occupational tests and were currently registered with a test publisher or had completed a previously recognized training course.)

• have had their assessment practices verified by the BPS.

For most people who wish to learn to use tests, the new process is not all that different from the preceding practice. They will attend a training course run by a Chartered Psychologist who is qualified to assess their competence. By the completion of the training they will have had their competence in all seven areas assessed and will be qualified to use tests at this level. On successful completion of the course, people will be able to apply to the BPS for their Certificate of Competence in Occupational Testing (Level A). The British Psychological Society charges £50 for the award of each certificate. (The fee is waived for Chartered Psychologists with a current Practising Certificate.) There is an optional £15 a year charge for having your name added to the Register of Competence in Occupational Testing maintained by the BPS. To purchase tests, potential

---

Figure 9.2 Example of some elements from Unit 5: Administering tests to one or more candidates and dealing with scoring procedures

Does the Assessee:

☐ plan test sessions with due regard to the maximum number of candidates who can be assessed in one session and the maximum duration of each session?

☐ ensure that any equipment (e.g. computer) is operating correctly and that sufficient test materials are available for use by the candidate?

☐ ensure, where re-useable materials are being used, that they are carefully checked for marks and notes which may have been made by previous candidates?

☐ brief candidates on the purpose of the test session and put them at ease while maintaining an appropriately businesslike atmosphere?

☐ enter the candidate's personal details in the test session log, together with relevant details of what assessment instruments were used, etc?

☐ check to ensure that all candidates have the necessary materials?

☐ use standard test instructions and present them clearly and intelligibly to the candidates?

☐ provide candidates with sufficient time to work through example test items?

---

test users will need to register with a test publisher who will want evidence of their competence (normally the Certificate of Competence).

Most of the major test publishers run their own training courses, but training courses are also run by other Chartered Psychologists. Training is also provided by some educational institutions as part of their short course programmes or as part of longer courses (such as an MSc in Occupational Psychology, or a Diploma in Careers Guidance). However, the extent to which this training is recognized by test publishers may vary.

The intention of this approach to certification is to produce much clearer accountability for training. Chartered Psychologists who certify competence could be in breach of their professional code of conduct, and liable to disciplinary action, if they certify people as competent who turn out not to be so. The focus on demonstrating competence also marks a shift of emphasis from attending training courses to the successful completion of training. It recognizes also that competence can be achieved in a variety of ways. Organizations that employ appropriately qualified Chartered Psychologists may devise their own in-house training programmes. These might be structured very differently from the typical five-day course provided by a test publisher or other trainer.

When this approach to training was being devised, it was hoped that the Certificate of Competence (or the equivalent Statement) would be recognized by all test publishers as evidence for competence in the use of any test that fell within its remit. In practice, because any particular course can only introduce people to a relatively small number of tests, test publishers may require people who possess the Certificate of Competence to undergo further training before they will register them to use their tests, or to use some specific tests that they sell. There is a certain logic to this. Few people can claim that they can pick up all they need to know about using a test from just reading a test manual. Test publishers are naturally concerned to minimize any risk that their tests are brought into disrepute by inappropriate use. They attempt to control the use of their own test materials by making people have at least a minimum amount of specific training in their use. Typically this means that, if someone has the Certificate or Statement of Competence in Occupational Testing based on the training they have received on one publisher's tests, they would have to attend a conversion course, usually of one or two days' duration, to become qualified to use another publisher's tests. However, critics might argue that this training is something of a money spinner for the test publishers, who are effectively implying that certification based on someone else's tests does not provide the level or quality of training that they require.

The success of this new approach to training is dependent on its widespread acceptance. It is encouraging that it has been endorsed by the Institute of Personnel and Development (IPD). They have revised their *Code on Psychological Testing* to state that only holders of the Level A Certificate or Statement of Competence in Occupational Testing should use tests. It is also supported by the leading UK test publishers.

Quality control is important to any training and accreditation system. For this system, quality control is maintained by a team of verifiers who are responsible to the BPS for accrediting the Chartered Psychologists who in turn affirm people for their Certificates. At the same time, the BPS has also published guidance for assessors (Steering Committee on Test Standards, 1992, 1994) and published an open learning programme (Bartram and Lindley, 1994) as a resource for people wanting to learn to use tests.

Level B: Personality assessment

In the past, the use of many personality measures was restricted to psychologists. Non-psychologists were only able to become trained in the use of a relatively small number of personality measures. In the last few years, more and more personality measures have come on to the market and there has been increased interest among non-psychologists in using these measures. As a result, the new competence-based approach to psychological testing is in the process of being extended to the area of personality assessment. However, because of the complexity of personality assessment, the standards for Level B are structured differently. There will be both an Intermediate Level B Certificate and a Full Level B Certificate. The nine units of competence that have been identified for Level B are broken down into three sub-groups:

- foundation knowledge (2 units)
- test use (3 units)
- test choice and evaluation (4 units).

The Intermediate Level B Certificate is intended for people with foundation knowledge and expertise in the use of at least one personality measure. It covers the two units of foundation knowledge and the three units of test use. The Full Level B Certificate will be available to people with both a broader and more in-depth knowledge and expertise in the use of a number of personality measures. It will be awarded to people who have been trained in the use of more than one personality measure and have also completed the four units concerned with test choice and evaluation.

Units 1 and 2 make up the Foundation Units and focus on the broad range of assessment issues relating to personality. They cover the basic knowledge and general understanding required to use personality measures.

Units 3, 4 and 5 are concerned with test use. They deal with test administration, interpretation and feedback, respectively. (Evidence of competence in the use of one personality measure is required for the Intermediate Level B Certificate and in the use of at least two different instruments for the Full Level B Certificate.)

Units 6 to 9 are concerned with test choice and evaluation. These units are required only for the Full Level B Certificate. Units 6 and 7 deal with measurement issues, test construction, reliability and validity as they apply to personality measures. Issues concerned with computer-based assessment are dealt with in unit 8 and issues to do with the limitations of personality measures and an understanding of the situations where it is appropriate to use them are dealt with in unit 9.

The BPS Steering Committee on Test Standards recognizes that, in an ideal world, users of personality measures should be competent to use a variety of different instruments. If they use only one, there is a danger that the test users will think they can use the same test in all situations. In practice, it takes time to acquire and develop expertise in an instrument. It would be hard to stop test users using measures they have been judged competent to use. This led the Steering Committee to propose an Intermediate Level B Certificate for users who have been trained on a single instrument. However, it is to be hoped that many users will want to progress from the Intermediate Level B to the Full Level B Certificate.

Training in the use of the main personality measures has previously involved an initial training course (5 days), or conversion course (3 days), with a follow-up day three to four months later. At the follow-up day, participants present case studies and have the quality of their work reviewed. Users are not considered to be fully competent until they have successfully completed the follow-up day. Publishers are still developing training courses for the new Level B Intermediate and Full Certificates but it is to be expected that a similar model will be adopted as far as the test use training component is concerned.

The relationship between Level A and Level B

Level B is not designed as an alternative to Level A. Rather it is intended to build on Level A training. Possessing the Level A Certificate or Statement of Competence in Occupational Testing is, therefore, a pre-requisite for Level B training. Training at Level B is broader and, while not formally repeating elements of Level A, may review aspects of Level A work that need to be reconsidered for the wider range of testing that is covered by Level B. Figure 9.3 sets out the structure of the qualification system and is designed to show how a user's level of competence in using tests will increase when moving from Level A through the Intermediate Level B to the Full Level B Certificate.

Maintaining skill

Clearly, to maintain a skill it needs to be used, and the quality of that skill needs to be reviewed and updated periodically. Seminars and workshops on aspects of testing are held regularly at major conferences for psycho-

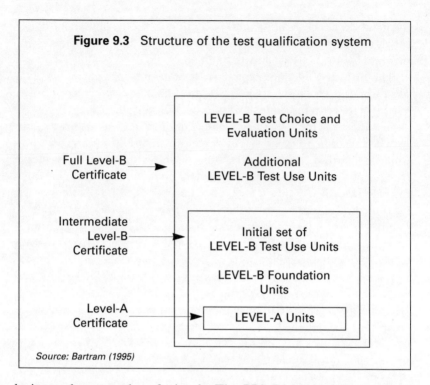

Figure 9.3 Structure of the test qualification system

Source: Bartram (1995)

logists and personnel professionals. The BPS Division of Occupational Psychology runs Continuing Professional Development events, some of which address issues concerned with testing and assessment.

Professional journals in personnel management and psychology regularly feature articles on developments in testing and assessment. *Selection and Development Review* is a journal published by the BPS and sent to all people on the Register of Competence in Occupational Testing. Test publishers also run one-off events on aspects of testing, for example equal opportunities issues, and commercial conference organizers also regularly run events that focus on the use of tests (sometimes in conjunction with a test publisher). Test publishers are also regular exhibitors at conferences. Many major personnel and management conferences have exhibitions attached to them.

It is, however, surprising that there are not more test user groups. These exist in many other areas (such as computing). The idea of a test user group is that it would hold meetings and/or publish a newsletter, where users of a particular test could share information and their experience of using it. There is tremendous value in hearing in detail about someone else's experience of using a test – what they like about it, what they dislike about it, and so on. User groups could provide an invaluable source of information for potential test users.

At present there is in the UK a 16PF Users Group and the British Association for Psychological Type for users of the Myers-Briggs Type Indicator. The 16PF User group runs about five educational events a year and also publishes a newsletter. The British Association for Psychological Type also produces a newsletter and runs workshops. It has an Annual Conference and there are nine local groups which hold their own meetings. Information about how to find out more about these two groups is given in Sources of further information (page 162).

Understanding psychological testing – a review

The need for this book has been stimulated by the rapid growth in psychological testing and the increased interest in all aspects of testing. As the use of tests becomes more widespread, testing affects more people. This results in the need for more people to have a basic understanding of psychological testing. In addition to providing basic information on how tests are used, this book has aimed to set out the main stages in becoming a qualified test user. The sequence of stages in becoming a test user might run as follows.

1. You might want to use tests

If you are interested in using tests, then the first few chapters aim to provide introductory information about tests. It is essential to understand some basic information if you are to use tests in a considered manner and to understand their benefits and limitations. This includes learning about:

• the reasons for using tests and types of decisions that tests are used for

• how the widespread use of tests led to the need to evaluate tests

• the importance of standardization and objectivity as a goal for testing

• the main types of psychological tests and the implications of recent developments in testing (such as the use of computers) for the assessment process

• the applications of tests in occupational and organizational settings, such as personnel selection, career counselling and the use of tests for training and personal development

• the use of tests in education and elsewhere

- promoting self-understanding as one of the goals of all testing.

With an understanding of these issues, you will be able to decide whether it is appropriate to use tests for the decision-making situation you are considering.

Developing some initial insight into why and where tests are used is the first stage of any decision to become a test user. Once you have reflected on that decision, and decided that you want to investigate the possibility of using tests further, it is time to move on to the next stage.

2. Proper use of tests

Understanding how tests are used properly is the next stage in becoming a qualified user. This means knowing about:

- how to use tests appropriately, for example explaining why tests are being used and how the information from the test session will be used

- how to administer and score tests, including knowing about common scoring systems and how to interpret test results and provide feedback to candidates

- the professional responsibilities of the test user

- the importance of the key measurement concepts, such as treating scores as estimates, and of understanding the meaning of reliability and validity to test use

- being aware how other factors besides the testing process itself can affect the use of tests

- concerns relating to fairness and equality of opportunity in using tests

- the importance of monitoring all stages of selection processes

- the limitations of testing.

3. Finding out about tests

Once the desire to use tests has been confirmed and you are aware of the issues involved in the proper use of tests, the next stage is to start doing some serious work on finding out about possible tests that you could use. Chapter 8 sets out the issues that need to be considered. At this stage the main tasks are really about collecting information about specific tests, how they are made available, what level of training is required to use them and so on. Sources of information that you might want to consult include:

- test publishers and their catalogues
- test manuals
- test reviews
- other test users
- expert advice.

The general issues involved in evaluating these sources of information are discussed in Chapter 8. Underlying concerns here are the technical nature of much of the information and the difficulty of getting impartial advice. It is generally best to consult widely at this stage; extra time spent in the collecting and reviewing of information is likely to pay dividends later. In so far as test publishing is a competitive marketplace, different publishers produce tests that are intended to compete with each other and, while not necessarily equivalent from a technical point of view, are designed for similar target populations and similar purposes. It is worth examining the catalogues of more than one publisher as well as test reviews.

4. Getting trained

Using tests requires training. At this stage the choice of where to get trained will be influenced by any decision that has already been made about the tests that you want to use. Bearing in mind that the major test publishers now usually require that anyone wanting to use their tests must receive some additional training from them, even if they already hold the Level A Certificate or Statement of Competence in Occupational Testing, it might appear to make sense to receive training directly from the test publisher who publishes the tests you want to use.

One potential danger is that, for fairly obvious reasons, test publishers train primarily in the tests that they sell. Without intending any criticism of any single test publisher, it is hard to believe that any one test publisher would publish the best tests for all situations. While some test users might find that all their test needs can be met by one supplier, others will find that they need to become registered with more than one publisher and this will almost certainly mean receiving some additional training from each publisher in the use of their particular tests. The risk for test users is that they become locked into one test supplier and perhaps, at some future date when they are reviewing their testing needs, do not look at the offerings from other publishers.

5. Extend and maintain skill

Once you are qualified, tests can be purchased and used. This requires formally registering with the test publisher. Further training from other publishers, or in personality assessment, may be required if you want to extend the range of tests you wish to use.

Riding a bicycle may be a skill that once learnt is never forgotten. However, other skills need to be maintained. Skills in psychological testing need to be reviewed and updated as well. Advantage should be taken of seminars and workshops on testing in order to keep skills and knowledge up to date. These also provide opportunities for networking and learning about new developments in testing practice.

Promoting best practice

To the outsider it might appear that psychological testing is highly regulated and that to gain access to tests requires the potential users to go through a long and expensive process of training, certification and registration before they are able to buy and use tests. However, this book has tried to set out some of the reasons why a free market in psychological tests is not a desirable alternative and to highlight why there is a need for regulation.

It is probably worthwhile to summarize the key advantages that regulation offers to test users and test takers. It means that:

- Test takers can be confident that test users have been trained and certified as competent to administer and interpret the tests they use. It represents, therefore, an important safeguard of their rights.

- Test users are aware of the full range of their responsibilities in relation to using tests appropriately. It provides processes to inform test users about issues involved in psychological testing and helps them to be more critical consumers in an increasingly complex marketplace.

More generally, regulation in any market can be seen as an attempt to make sure that minimum standards of practice are adhered to. It cannot guarantee that bad practice will not occur but it helps to minimize the risk. This has benefits for test takers, test users and organizations and individuals who are making decisions on the basis of test results.

While there are many issues to do with psychological testing that psychologists and others may disagree about, there is a broad consensus that regulation has significant benefits. The present system that has been developed over the last ten years is seen as superior to the one that it replaces in being more straightforward to operate, and fairer in that it treats all potential users of tests equally.

One word of warning – the present regulatory scheme is voluntary. It is effectively binding on Chartered Psychologists and most, if not all, of the leading test publishers have agreed to use it. There are, however, other people selling tests outside the scheme. They may run their own training schemes and maintain a register of people qualified to use their tests; or they may just sell tests that they have developed to anyone who comes along. The need to be an informed and critical consumer remains.

A final word

As a result of reading this book, I hope that potential test users – and those reading just for general interest – will be more aware of the wide range of issues that need to be considered when moving through the stages from thinking about using a test in a particular situation to the end point of using that test and acting on the test results. If tests are used responsibly, they provide a way of helping decision-making to be both more effective and fairer. Irresponsible use, however, threatens not only the value of particular tests, or the use of tests in particular circumstances, but the position of psychological testing as a whole.

Guide for Test Takers

Charles Jackson and Ann Turner

Most of us have been asked to complete a psychological test at one time or another. Many of us will be asked to complete a psychological test at some time in the future. Even if we are never required to take a psychological test, we will probably know other people who are taking tests, such as our partners, children, friends or work colleagues, who might well ask for our advice about completing them. What should we tell them and what would it be useful for us to know ourselves, just in case we are asked to complete a psychological test?

This brief guide aims to demystify the process by answering some of the most common questions that people ask. It focuses on paper-and-pencil tests that are designed for group administration and does not cover other forms of assessment such as interviews or assessment centres. In order to keep this guide relatively brief, references are made to other chapters in the book where issues are discussed in more detail.

Q1 – When are tests used?

For the test takers this question is about the situations in which they are likely to be asked to take tests (see Chapter 4 for a fuller discussion of where tests are used). Some the main areas where tests are used include:

In Education – Schools and colleges use tests to assess students. Assessment may be carried out as part of the selection process, or to allocate students to appropriate classes when they first enter the school or college. Tests are also used to assess the outcomes of learning and for guidance purposes (see below).

At Work – Employers frequently use tests as part of their selection processes. Increasingly, tests are also used at work to measure things such as learning style or to help work teams and individuals gain insight as part of development activities or a coaching process.

For Guidance – Psychological tests are often used to assist people to understand themselves as part of guidance and counselling activities. In these circumstances the test taker is also the main consumer of the test results.

Q2 – What tests are most commonly used?

It is possible to distinguish two types of test – those that have right and wrong answers and those that come with the instruction 'There are no right and wrong answers'. The former are commonly referred to as tests of ability but more correctly as tests of maximum performance. The latter, which include measures of personality and interest inventories, are called measures of typical response. Measures of typical response (usually called 'measures' rather than tests just because there are no right and wrong answers), are based on self-report, that is on individuals describing how they typically behave, their likes and dislikes, and so on.

Q3 – How are test results interpreted?

Psychological tests should be used only by people who have been trained to use them. They are likely to be useful only if they are carefully administered and interpreted. The results from most tests will be interpreted in relation to the performance of other people on the same tests and relevant information about the person tested. Some tests, several interest inventories for example, use information only from the person who has taken the test to make comparisons between that individual's preferences for different sorts of activity.

Ability tests – tests of maximum performance

Q4 – What are tests of maximum performance?

On tests of maximum performance the best score is the highest score, and this is achieved by getting as many questions correct as possible. These tests require maximum effort from the test taker. Some tests are timed which means there is pressure on the test taker to work quickly.

Testing ability has been a popular exercise throughout the 20th century. Ability has been defined in many different ways and tests have been devised to measure performance against these different definitions. Recently, there has been a move away from the belief that tests can measure intellectual capacity, independently of acquired understanding and emotion. Test results these days are more likely to be accepted as some indication of the individual's current capacity to solve different sorts of problems.

There are an enormous number of ability tests in use, some measuring specific aptitudes (such as speed and accuracy at clerical tasks, mechanical ability, manipulative ability) and others measuring different aspects of verbal, numerical and spatial ability (see Chapter 3). Some employers, for example the Civil Service, have developed their own tests.

Most tests designed to measure general ability give scores on verbal ability, numerical ability and spatial ability and include these three types of items, possibly in separate sections of a single test. Figure A.1 shows some of the different styles that might be used for items under these three headings.

Important points to bear in mind when you are taking such a test:

Key Point 1 – Make sure you understand the example items
Before starting most tests you will be given the opportunity to complete a series of examples (sometimes called practice items). These examples are of the same order of difficulty as the early items in the test itself. It is important that you understand the principle behind the solution to each type of problem. If you have any difficulty understanding why the correct answer is correct, you should ask for help from the person administering the test. Do not be embarrassed about asking for help. The examples are there to make sure you 'get your eye in' and any difficulty you have in working out the examples simply reflects the fact that you have not yet done so. The importance of understanding the principle behind the examples cannot be emphasized too much. If you allow embarrassment to stop you sorting out queries about the examples, you will be doing yourself a great disservice.

Key Point 2 – Be clear about time limits and work at an appropriate speed
Once you are ready to start on the test itself you will be informed how long you have to complete the test. (There should be no time limit on how long you spend on completing the examples.) People rarely complete any ability test within the time limit. It is important to settle on a compromise between working carefully to avoid unnecessary errors and to maximize the likelihood of correct solutions, and working quickly, identifying and leaving questions that you feel you are not going to be able to solve. Do not spend time checking answers. Go on through the test as carefully and quickly as you can.

Figure A.1 Examples of Ability Test Items

Verbal items:

1. Vocabulary (e.g. Which word is similar in meaning to *prevail*?
   Restrict Predominate Earlier Values)

2. Opposites (e.g. The opposite of *us* is ....)

3. Classification (e.g. Which word on the right completes the set on the left?
   House Igloo Hut ....   Shop Library Wigwam)

4. Meaning (e.g. Sort out these words into a meaningful sentence:
   the fell the ground to bee)

5. Précis (e.g. Summarize the main points of a paragraph in 100 words)

Numerical items:

1. Percentages (e.g. Express 25 out of 50 as a percentage)

2. Ratios (e.g. 60:40 is the same as 6:__)

3. Decimals (e.g. Multiply 0.2 by 0.6)

4. Fractions (e.g. Add 1/3 to 1/6)

5. Interpretation of graphs (e.g. From a graph showing a company's profits over a 10-year period, state the profit made in the 6th year)

6. Summarize information presented in tables (e.g. From a list of fluctuating oil prices over a 10-year period, state the average price)

Spatial items:

1. Pattern completion (e.g. Choose the piece of jigsaw to complete a picture pattern)

2. Shape matching (e.g. Choose the mirror image of a diagram)

3. 2-dimensions into 3-dimensions (e.g. Which coloured box would be made from a flat picture provided?)

4. Rotation (e.g. Which view shows what a figure would look like when rotated through 60 degrees?)

Key Point 3 – Some items are very difficult

In most tests the items get harder as you go through the test or subtest. Remember, most ability tests will contain some items that are designed to be difficult for even extremely bright people. You will almost certainly find some of the questions extremely difficult. Try not to let this worry you.

Figure A.2 Variety of Practice Items: Questions

NOTE: *All examples have been invented and do not appear in any test.*

1. *Verbal*

(a) Identifying the order in a jumbled series:

Which is the middle item of the series?   lake puddle ocean pool sea

(b) Recognizing the relationship between verbal items:

When is to *where* as *time* is to: (a) clock   (b) appointment
                                          (c) meeting (d) place

(c) Recognizing the relationship between concepts:

Which word on the right bears a similar relation to the two words on the left?

cottage Caerphilly   garden mountain cheese castle

2. *Numerical*

(d) Recognizing sequences in numbers:
Which number is missing from the following series?   1 2 _ 3 3 3 4 4 4 4

(e) Recognizing the relationship between numerical items:

2 is to 10 as 5 is to: 10   50   5   25

(f) 'Simple' arithmetic:

If a cyclist travels at 9 mph and leaves home at 5 o'clock what time does he arrive at a pub 31.5 miles away. (It is not sufficient to say before closing time!)

3. *Diagrammatic*

(g) Recognizing how shapes are changing:
Which shape on the right comes next in the sequence on the left?

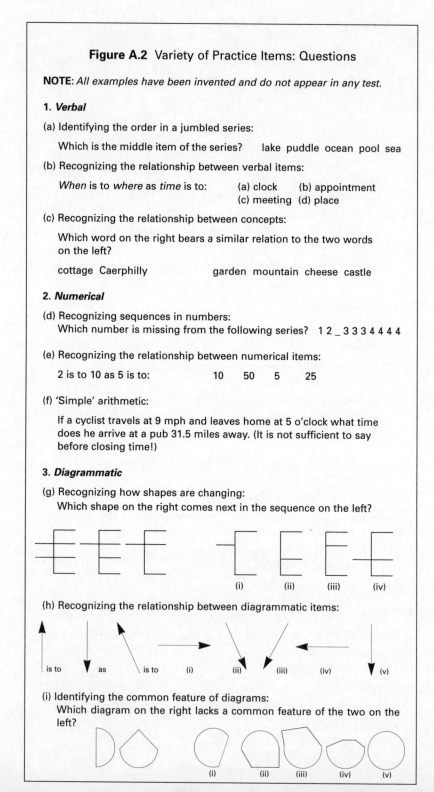

(h) Recognizing the relationship between diagrammatic items:

(i) Identifying the common feature of diagrams:
Which diagram on the right lacks a common feature of the two on the left?

Figure A.2 presents some example questions. The answers are given in Figure A.5 at the end of this guide.

Tests of logical thinking, verbal analysis and evaluation of arguments

There are a number of tests that, instead of consisting of single questions which the person taking the test has to answer, require the test taker to read a passage and then answer a number of questions about it. Such tests are quite widely used for selecting people such as university graduates for managerial, technical and professional jobs.

One test that falls into this category and is quite widely used in the UK is called the Watson-Glaser Critical Thinking Appraisal. This test is described in more detail in Figure A.3 but there are a number of other tests on the market that adopt a similar approach to testing ability.

The Watson-Glaser Critical Thinking Appraisal has clear instructions and fully explained examples of all the types of problem presented. As with all tests, it is important to read all the material carefully before tackling the problems themselves. The problems sometimes deal with topics about which you may have strong opinions. It is important that you answer according to the criteria provided, regardless of your own personal beliefs. One purpose of this test and other similar tests is see whether your ability to think logically is affected by your attitude toward the content of the questions.

The Watson-Glaser Critical Thinking Appraisal is sometimes presented as a timed exercise. You will either be told that you have 40 minutes to complete the test or that you have as much time as necessary. If you have particular difficulty with a question or series of questions, go on to another question. The logic of statements often falls into place more easily if you come back to particularly troublesome items after time spent tackling other problems.

Q5 – What are Tests of Maximum Performance used for?

- *Selection* – Widely used by employers to help select people for jobs; by schools and colleges to select potential students.

- *Attainment/Placement* – Used to measure skills and knowledge, and to place people in appropriate education and training programmes.

- *Guidance and counselling* – Used in guidance and counselling, and as part of development activities to promote self-insight and understanding.

Figure A.3 The Watson-Glaser Critical Thinking Appraisal

This test has five sections, each concerned with different types of problems. The sections are:

1. *Inferences.* Inferences are the conclusions drawn from presented facts. If you lie in bed in the morning and hear the sound of cars travelling on wet streets, you may infer that it is or has been raining. You are probably correct, but could be wrong – there could be a burst water main. The first series of problems in the Watson-Glaser Critical Thinking Appraisal investigates ability to make correct inferences from information provided. A situation is described in detail and you have to decide how likely it is that each of a series of inferences is true.

2. *Recognition of Assumptions.* In this section you have to identify the assumptions made in a series of brief statements. For example: 'I'll see you when I get back at 6 o'clock tonight' assumes the speaker will get back at 6 o'clock and that the person addressed will be there.

3. *Deductions.* Here you have to recognize which conclusions are true, that is, follow logically from a series of statements, and which are false and do not follow. For example, given the statements (premises):

   'Everyone likes to go on holiday'
   'Many people prefer to holiday abroad'

   you would have to decide whether or not it follows that:

   'Some people prefer to holiday in their own country' (True)
   'Some people prefer not to go on holiday' (False)

4. *Interpretation.* In this section a judgement has to be made about whether or not a conclusion follows logically from the case presented in a brief descriptive paragraph.

   For example:
   '30% of mathematicians graduating from Manchester University in 1985 went on to study for higher degrees there. Only 5% of mathematicians graduating from Bristol University in the same year stayed on there to do higher degrees.'

   It would be correct to interpret these data as showing that, in 1985, a greater proportion of Manchester maths graduates than Bristol maths graduates remained in their own institutions to do postgraduate work.

   It would not be correct to interpret the data as showing more Manchester maths graduates went on to do higher degrees than did Bristol maths graduates. (Bristol graduates may have moved to other universities to do postgraduate work, or there may be many more maths graduates at Bristol.)

5. *Evaluation of Arguments.* Here you have to decide which of a series of arguments are strong – that is, important and directly related to a question – and which are weak. The exercises consist of a question followed by a series of supporting or opposing arguments which have to be classified as strong or weak. For example:

   Question: 'Should children be offered free nursery schooling from the age of 3?'

   Answer: 'Yes; children gain long-term educational advantage from nursery school.' (Strong argument)

   Answer: 'Yes, children enjoy playing with their peers from the age of 3.' (Weak argument)

Q6 – Should I guess?

If you are unsure which answer to choose to some questions on ability tests, it is advisable to guess. It is usually possible to rule out some of the potential answers on a multiple choice test as incorrect thus increasing the probability that your guess will be correct.

Q7 – Will practice make perfect?

Ability testing is unfair if people are not able to perform to the best of their ability. Therefore, best professional advice states that people should be given the opportunity to practise before they have to take tests. Most tests have example items for just this reason. For many people completing these will be sufficient but for others additional familiarization and practice will at least reduce the stress of testing.

If you have never taken an ability test before and/or finished your education a long time ago, some practice will probably improve your performance. Some organizations make available practice tests for just this purpose, because testing is really only fair if everybody taking the tests is able to perform to the best of their ability. If you fall into this category, you may find it useful to look at one or other of the books listed on page 156. These contain practice items and tests as well as offering more extensive advice on testing.

People applying for several jobs, for example graduates leaving university, often report being asked to take the same test more than once in a short space of time. Almost certainly they will gain some slight advantage from this. They will remember some of the answers that they gave, or the style of the questions, and this is likely to mean, for example on a timed test, that they have an advantage over people who have not completed the test before. They will be able to spend a little more time on the more difficult items. In most cases the improvement in performance will be slight but, of course, if they then score just above the cut-off point, the benefit in getting through to the next stage of the selection process, or even being offered the job, is immeasurable. No system can be perfect. The reason organizations use tests for selection purposes is to improve the probability of selecting people who can do the job, but no process can guarantee that the best person will get the job. Some organizations, for example the Civil Service, will not allow people to take their tests a second time until at least a six-month gap has elapsed.

Q8 – Will testing involve computers?

Traditionally, most psychological tests were paper-and-pencil exercises. Nowadays, however, many tests are being conducted by computer. Questions are presented on the screen and you have to type in your reply or hit the appropriate letter or number key to indicate which from the list of possible answers you think is correct or applies to you. Probably one of the most obvious differences from conventional testing is that you cannot easily skip items and then go back to them later.

Computers offer many advantages to the tester, for example making scoring easier. However, it is not straightforward to turn the paper-and-pencil version of a test into a computer-based version (see Chapter 3).

Personality Questionnaires and Measures of Typical Response

Q9 – What are Measures of Typical Response?

Measures of typical response are closer to what many people expect a psychological test to be. However, they are really just tools to help describe some aspects of the person on a set of dimensions, for example occupational interests, using a framework that has been specially designed for this purpose.

They are questionnaires designed for self-completion, and they will have written instructions that are usually self-explanatory. These tests are untimed and you are expected to answer all the questions.

Two main types of psychological test come under this heading:

- measures of occupational interests and values

- measures to assess personality.

Q10 – What are Measures of Occupational Interests and Values?

These are questionnaires (often called inventories) that are used primarily to assist people in making career decisions. They are used by people giving careers advice and counselling, either on a one-to-one basis, or with groups of people in workshops. Their purpose is to help people identify work areas that may be of interest to them. The content of such measures is usually clearly work-related. It might cover work activities, school subjects liked or disliked, preferences for different jobs, and so on. The different measures report scores in various ways. Some compare an individual's answers with those of people in a variety of occupations, effectively reporting a similarity score that shows how similar the person taking the test is to people already working in each occupation. Others report scores on a set of interest dimensions. These can then be related to known interest profiles for particular occupations. Some tests combine both approaches.

These measures are used to promote self-understanding. They are used primarily in guidance settings and sometimes also in organizational settings as part of learning and development activities. Even if people are not planning to change jobs, interest inventories and related measures of work values or needs can be useful in helping people identify their niche in a particular occupational or organizational setting.

Q11 – How do we assess personality?

Personality assessment is an area of some controversy. Any measure directed at quantifying dimensions of personality assumes that such dimensions are stable and that behaviour is consistent over a range of situations. Clearly, these underlying assumption can be challenged. A further difficulty arises from the fact that questions in personality questionnaires are deliberately somewhat ambiguous. For example: 'Do you perform tasks quickly?' begs the questions: 'What tasks?' 'What does quickly mean?' 'When?' etc.

It is worth bearing in mind when faced with personality questionnaires that they are to a certain extent relatively crude measures and should be answered as such. There is no point in worrying about the generalizations you will be making when completing the questionnaire. The person looking at your answers will be as aware as you of the limitations of the questionnaire.

Measures of personality are not only used to select people for jobs. They are also widely used to promote self-understanding – for example, in counselling and guidance and for such activities as giving members of a work group insight into each other's personal styles.

The Sixteen Personality Factor Questionnaire (16PF) is described in Figure A.4, but there are other personality measures that are also widely used in selecting people for jobs. In the UK these include: the California Psychological Inventory (CPI); the Eysenck Personality Profiler (EPP); and the Occupational Personality Questionnaire (OPQ). Note that these measures are also widely used for other purposes and their use is not restricted to selecting people for jobs.

Although these measures use a variety of question formats and report scores on different personality dimensions, the underlying rationale of these measures of personality is the same. Your best approach to any

Figure A.4 Sixteen Personality Factor Questionnaire (16PF)

The 16PF, so called because it produces information on sixteen personality dimensions, is a commonly used personality questionnaire. To each question there are three possible answers and there are over 180 questions on the form of the test most frequently used. You are expected to work quickly and give 'first responses'. The sixteen factors are summarized here by key words and somewhat crude, fictitious examples. In the actual test, each dimension is 'measured' by a number of items, randomly presented. The sixteen dimensions measured by the 16PF can be summarized as:

1. Reserved : Outgoing. *Question*: Would you rather be:
   (a) a barman   (b) uncertain   (c) a hermit

2. More intelligent : Less intelligent. An intelligence type of item.

3. Emotional : Calm. *Question*: I lose my temper over minor incidents.
   (a) True   (b) In between   (c) False

4. Humble : Assertive. *Question*: In arguments, I always feel others are correct and I am wrong.
   (a) Often   (b) Occasionally   (c) Never

5. Serious : Happy-go-lucky. *Question*: You should always sleep on any decision.
   (a) True   (b) Uncertain   (c) False

6. Expedient: Conscientious. *Question*: I double-check for errors when I perform calculations.
   (a) Always   (b) Sometimes   (c) Never

7. Shy: Uninhibited. Question: I like giving practical demonstrations in front of others.
   (a) True   (b) Uncertain   (c) False

8. Tough-minded : Tender-minded. *Question*: The end justifies the means.
   (a) Yes   (b) Sometimes   (c) No

9. Trusting : Suspicious. *Question*: It is asking for trouble not to have a burglar alarm on your house.
   (a) True   (b) Uncertain   (c) False

10. Practical: Imaginative. *Question*: Would you rather:
    (a) mend a bike   (b) in between   (c) tell a story

11. Forthright: Calculating. *Question*: You should always agree with your boss in public.
    (a) Yes   (b) In between   (c) No

12. Self-assured: Apprehensive. *Question*: I never expect to get the job I apply for.
    (a) True   (b) Uncertain   (c) False

13. Conservative: Radical. *Question*: Old values are usually the best values.
    (a) True   (b) Uncertain   (c) False

14. Group membership : Self-sufficiency. *Question*: I always ask what others think before stating an opinion.
    (a) True   (b) In between   (c) False

15. Undisciplined : Controlled. *Question*: If I have planned to study, I never let myself be distracted.
    (a) True   (b) In between   (c) False

16. Relaxed : Tense. *Question*: I can always forget about worries completely in social situations.
    (a) Yes   (b) Uncertain   (c) No

personality measure is to suspend judgement and just get on with completing it as quickly and as honestly as possible.

Other questionnaires that are used to measure personality include:

- the Minnesota Multiphasic Personality Inventory (MMPI) which is mainly used for screening purposes in clinical settings, or to screen people for high-risk, high-stress occupations where emotional stability is important.

- the Myers-Briggs Type Indicator (MBTI) which is designed to help people discover, understand and appreciate their personal style and is widely used for leadership training, team building and counselling purposes.

Q12 – Surely there are right answers?

In some situations it may appear that despite the instructions that assure us 'there are no right and wrong answers', some answers would be better than others. This applies particularly when a personality measure is being completed as part of a selection process. However tempting it may be to try to present the personality profile you feel is most desirable, in practice the best advice is to answer honestly. Usually completing a personality measure is only one part of the selection process. You should consider whether it will be possible, or even worthwhile, to maintain a deception throughout other stages of the selection process. Ask yourself: 'Will I benefit from getting a job for which I am not really suited?'

Although it is probably possible on most personality measures to bias one's answers in a certain direction, it is worth knowing that most of the widely used personality measures have scales to detect people who are trying to distort their replies. These work by looking at consistency of response or by noting when people give extremely unusual replies, for example saying no to the question: 'Have you ever told a lie?'

Q13 – Will I get any feedback on my test results?

You should receive some information on your test performance. There should be at least some oral feedback. Good professional practice will provide you with a written report and the opportunity to discuss the meaning of your test results (see Chapter 7). The person who gives you feedback should be a qualified user of the test that you have completed. This is normally the one time in the testing process that test takers get a chance to:

- report any special circumstances that may have affected their test performance

- enquire about the group with which their results are being compared (for example, people of the same gender, education level, occupational group, or ethnic background)

- comment on whether they think the test results are a fair reflection of their abilities or description of their personality.

It is appropriate for the test taker to be assertive at this point and to address the issues listed above. If tests have been administered as part of a selection process, it is not reasonable to expect to be given careers counselling, or detailed reasons as to why the position was offered to someone else, as part of the feedback process. However, in other circumstances feedback may include guidance and counselling.

Q14 – Where can I obtain further information?

Many of the issues discussed here are dealt with in greater detail in earlier chapters of this book; relevant chapters have been listed in the text. Books that contain example tests that individuals can complete and score themselves include:

Byron, M. and Modha, S. (1991). *How to Master Selection Tests.* London: Kogan Page.
Barrett, J. and Williams, G. (1990). *Test Your Own Aptitude.* London: Kogan Page.
Eysenck, H. J. (1962). *Check Your Own IQ.* Harmondsworth: Penguin.
Eysenck, H. J. (1962). *Know Your Own IQ.* Harmondsworth: Penguin.
Eysenck, H. J. and Wilson, G. (1991). *Know Your Own Personality.* Harmondsworth: Penguin.

Figure A.5 Answers to practice items (see Figure A.2)

(a) lake (ocean sea lake pool puddle: decreasing area of water)
(b) place (*when* indicates a time, *where* indicates a place)
(c) cheese (cottage and Caerphilly are both types of cheese)
(d) 2 (one 1, two 2s, three 3s, four 4s etc.)
(e) 25 (2 multiplied by 5 equals 10; 5 multiplied by 5 equals 25)
(f) 8.30 (31.5 miles divided by 9 mph equals 3.5 hours. 5 o'clock plus 3.5 hours equals 8.30)
(g) (iii) (figure loses one outer stroke, then an inner. Next to go would be one more outer, leaving figure (iii))
(h) (ii) (arrows point in opposite direction)
(i) (v) (all the others have both straight and curved lines)

Appendix Figure 1 Calculating percentile scores

1. **Basic principles**
   If 200 people have taken a test and one person ranks 4th out of the 200, it follows that 196 people scored less than this person.

   Number scoring less: 200 − 4 = 196

   Percentile score (percentage scoring less): $\dfrac{196 \times 100}{200} = 98$

2. **Coping with ties**
   In reality, several people are likely to get the same score, so that in the group many people will have the same scores. The basic formula is modified to take account of this.

   The new formula is to calculate the number scoring less than the individual and add to this figure half the people scoring the same.

   If a person ranks 22nd out of 200 people who have taken the test and 6 people have the same score, the number scoring less:

   200 (total number of people) − 22 (individual rank) − 3 (half number of ties) = 175

   Percentile score: $\dfrac{175 \times 100}{200} = 87.5$

3. **Coping with large numbers**
   When a large number of people have taken a test it is easier to set out the results in a frequency table, calculate the cumulative frequency and then express this as a percentage.

   This involves the following stages:
   1. Identify the highest and lowest scores to calculate the score range.
   2. Divide the score range into equal score intervals (usually 15 plus) by choosing a class interval.
   3. Construct a frequency table by tallying the number in each class interval.
   4. Calculate a cumulative frequency distribution.
   5. Express this as a percentage.

   Normally this process would be done using a simple statistical program or spreadsheet on a computer.

Appendix Figure 2 Calculating standard scores

1. Calculate the mean (average score) by summing all the scores and dividing by the number of people (n) who took the test.

2. Calculate the standard deviation for the set of scores.

   a) Calculate for each person, their deviation from the mean.

      Deviation from mean (d) = X (raw score) – mean

   b) Square and sum deviations from mean = $d_1^2 + d_2^2 + d_3^2 \ldots + d_n^2 = N$

   c) Standard deviation (the square root of the **variance**) = $\sqrt{\dfrac{N}{n}}$

3. The standard score expresses each raw score as the number of standard deviations it is from the mean.

   Standard score (z score)   = $\dfrac{\text{raw score} - \text{mean}}{\text{standard deviation}}$

   For example assume the mean of a set of test scores is 55 and the standard deviation is 13.

   For a raw score of 75: $z = \dfrac{75 - 55}{13} = \dfrac{20}{13} = 1.5$

   For a raw score of 30 $z = \dfrac{30 - 55}{13} = \dfrac{-25}{13} = -1.9$

4. To convert z scores to a different scale, for example to T scores with a mean of 50 and a standard deviation of 10, multiply each z score by 10 and add to 50.

   For raw score of 75, z = 1.5; $T = 50 + (10 \times 1.5) = 65$

   For raw score of 30, z = – 1.9; $T = 50 + (10 \times -1.9) = 31$

Sources of further information

This is a short guide to sources of further information on psychological testing. For convenience, it is broken down into four sections:

- books
- test reviews
- user groups
- professional organizations.

Each section starts with a brief introduction to the material or information that is listed.

Books

This list includes classic textbooks by Cronbach and Anastasi which, although they are American, provide a detailed overview of the field and include descriptions of many tests. Fagan and VandenBos's book reviews the origins of psychology as an applied science. It contains two chapters, one by Anastasi and another by Landy, that are particularly good introductions to the history of testing. Gould's book provides a very readable but critical account of early testing programmes.

Two books in this list address the use of testing in particular settings. Seligman's book provides an excellent account of how psychological assessment and testing is used in career counselling and she includes descriptions of many tests that career counsellors might use. Managers' use of psychological tests is covered by Toplis *et al.*'s book. Bartram and Lindley provide a comprehensive study guide for those wanting to become qualified test users and Woodruffe's book is a very helpful introduction to the use of assessment centres.

Anastasi, A. (1988). *Psychological Testing* (6th Edition). New York: Macmillan.

Bartram, D. and Lindley, P. A. (1994). *Psychological Testing: The BPS Level A Open Learning Programme*. Leicester: BPS Books, The British Psychological Society.

Cronbach, L. J. (1990). *Essentials of Psychological Testing* (5th Edition). New York: Harper Collins.

Fagan, T. K. and VandenBos, G. R. (Eds) (1993). *Exploring Applied Psychology: Origins and Critical Analyses*. Washington: American Psychological Association.

Gould, S. J. (1981). *The Mismeasure of Man*. Harmondsworth: Penguin.

Seligman, L. (1994). *Developmental Career Counseling and Assessment* (2nd Edition). Thousand Oaks: Sage.

Toplis, J., Dulewicz, V. and Fletcher, C. (1991). *Psychological Testing: A Manager's Guide*. London: Institute of Personnel and Development.

Woodruffe, C. (1990). *Assessment Centres: Identifying and Developing Competence*. London: Institute of Personnel and Development.

Test reviews

Test reviews are a key source of further information on tests. This list covers current and up-to-date sources of reviews including those published by The British Psychological Society. Also listed are the latest *Mental Measurements Yearbooks* (*MMYs*) and their supplements. *Tests In Print IV* is a source book for further information on tests that contains descriptions of tests, references to journal articles about particular tests, and so on. It does not contain reviews but cross-refers to the *MMY* reviews. Landy's book presents original validation research rather than test reviews.

Bartram, D., Lindley, P. A. and Foster, J. M. (1990; 1992). *A Review of Psychometric Tests for Assessment in Vocational Training*. Leicester: BPS Books, The British Psychological Society.

Bartram, D., Anderson, N., Kellett, D., Lindley, P. A. and Robertson, I. (1995). *Review of Personality Assessment Instruments (Level B) for use in Occupational Settings*. Leicester: BPS Books, The British Psychological Society.

Conoley, J. C. and Impara, J. C. (Eds) (1994). *Supplement to the Eleventh Mental Measurements Yearbook*. Lincoln: University of Nebraska Press.

Conoley, J. C. and Impara, J. C. (Eds) (1995). *The Twelfth Mental Measurements Yearbook*. Lincoln: University of Nebraska Press.

Kramer, J. J. and Conoley, J. C. (Eds) (1992). *The Eleventh Mental Measurements Yearbook*. Lincoln: University of Nebraska Press.

Landy, F. J. (1992). *The Test Validity Yearbook: Organizational*. Hillsdale: Erlbaum.

Murphy, L. L., Conoley, J. C. and Impara, J. C. (Eds) (1994). *Tests In Print IV*. Lincoln: University of Nebraska Press.

User groups

Contact addresses for UK test user groups:

British Association for Psychological Type,
Emmaus House, Clifton Hill, Bristol BS8 4PD
Tel: 0117 946 6797   Fax: 0117 923 9508

Anne Watson, Membership Secretary, 16PF Users Group,
GNW Executive Search, Crown House, Hornbeam Square
North, Harrogate, North Yorkshire HG2 8PB
Tel: 01423 871770   Fax: 01423 872034

Professional organizations

Addresses for four professional organizations with an interest in psychological testing.

British Association for Counselling (BAC)
1 Regent Place, Rugby, Warwickshire CV21 2PJ
Tel: 01788 578328

The British Psychological Society (BPS),
St Andrews House, 48 Princess Road East, Leicester LE1 7DR
Tel: 0116 254 9568   Fax: 0116 247 0787

Institute of Careers Guidance
27a Lower High Street, Stourbridge, West Midlands DY8 1TA
Tel: 01384 376464

Institute of Personnel and Development (IPD),
IPD House, Camp Road, Wimbledon, London SW19 4UX
Tel: 0181 971 9000   Fax: 0181 263 3333

References

American Educational Research Association, American Psychological Association and National Council on Measurement in Education. (1985). *Standards for Educational and Psychological Testing.* Washington: American Psychological Association.

American Psychological Association. (1986). *Guidelines for Computer-based Tests and Interpretations.* Washington: American Psychological Association.

Anastasi, A. (1982). *Psychological Testing* (5th Edition). New York: Macmillan.

Banks, M. H., Jackson, P. R., Stafford, E. M. and Warr, P. B. (1982). *The Job Components Inventory Mark II: Training Studies.* Sheffield: Manpower Services Commission.

Baron, H. (1996). 'Strengths and limitations of ipsative measurement'. *Journal of Occupational and Organizational Psychology, 69,* 48-56.

Bartram, D. (1987). 'The development of an automated testing system for pilot selection: the MICROPAT project'. *Applied Psychology: An International Review, 36,* 279-98.

Bartram, D. (1995). 'The competence approach: the development of standards for the use of psychological tests in occupational settings'. *The Psychologist, 8,* 219-23.

Bartram, D. (1996). 'The relationship between ipsatized and normative measures of personality'. *Journal of Occupational and Organizational Psychology, 69,* 25-39.

Bartram, D., Lindley, P. A. and Foster, J. M. (1990; 1992). *A Review of Psychometric Tests for Assessment in Vocational Training.* Leicester: BPS Books, The British Psychological Society.

Bartram, D., Anderson, N., Kellett, D., Lindley, P. A. and Robertson, I. (1995). *Review of Personality Assessment Instruments (Level B) for use in Occupational Settings.* Leicester: BPS Books, The British Psychological Society.

Bartram, D. and Lindley, P. A. (1994). *Psychological Testing: The BPS Level A Open Learning Programme.* Leicester: BPS Books, The British Psychological Society.

Closs, S. J. (1996). 'On the factoring and interpretation of ipsative data'. *Journal of Occupational and Organizational Psychology, 69,* 41-7.

Conoley, J. C. and Impara, J. C. (Eds) (1994). *Supplement to the Eleventh Mental Measurements Yearbook.* Lincoln: University of Nebraska Press.

Conoley, J. C. and Impara, J. C. (Eds) (1995). *The Twelfth Mental Measurements Yearbook.* Lincoln: University of Nebraska Press.

Cronbach, L. J. (1970). *Essentials of Psychological Testing* (3rd Edition). New York: Harper and Row.

Cronbach, L. J. (1975). 'Five decades of public controversy over mental testing'. *American Psychologist, 30,* 1-13.

Cronbach, L. J. (1990). *Essentials of Psychological Testing* (5th Edition). New York: HarperCollins.

Dawis, R. V. (1992). 'The individual differences tradition in counseling psychology.' *Journal of Counseling Psychology, 39,* 7-19.

Downs, S., Farr, R. M. and Colbeck, L. (1978). 'Self-appraisal: a convergence of selection and guidance'. *Journal of Occupational Psychology, 51,* 271-278.

Eyde, L. D., Moreland, K. L. and Robertson, G. J. (1988). *Test user qualifications: a data-based approach to promoting good test use.* Washington: American Psychological Association.

Forer, B. R. (1949). 'The fallacy of personal validation: a class room demonstration of gullibility.' *Journal of Abnormal and Social Psychology, 44,* 118-23.

Hood, A. B. and Johnson, R. W. (1991). *Assessment in Counseling: a guide to the use of psychological assessment procedures.* Alexandria: American Association for Counseling and Development.

IPD (undated). *Code on Psychological Testing.* London: available from the Communications Department, Institute of Personnel and Development.

Jackson, C. and Yeates, J. (1993). *Development Centres: Assessing or Developing People?* Report 261. Brighton: Institute of Manpower Studies.

Kramer, J. J. and Conoley, J. C. (Eds) (1992). *The Eleventh Mental Measurements Yearbook.* Lincoln: University of Nebraska Press.

Landy, F. J. (1992). *The Test Validity Yearbook: Organizational.* Hillsdale: Erlbaum.

McCormick, E. J., Jeanneret, R. C. and Mecham, R. C. (1969). *Position Analysis Questionnaire.* West Lafayette, Indiana: Purdue Research Foundation.

Meehl, P. E. (1956). 'Wanted – A Good Cookbook'. *American Psychologist, 11,* 263-272.

Saville and Holdsworth Ltd. (1988). *The Work Profiling System Manual.* Esher: Saville and Holdsworth.

Stagner, R. (1958). 'The gullibility of personnel managers'. *Personnel Psychology,* Reprinted in Jackson, D. N. and Messick, S. (Eds) (1967). *Problems in Human Assessment.* New York: McGraw-Hill.

Steering Committee on Test Standards. (1992). *Certificate of Competence in Occupational Testing Level A: Guidance for Assessors.* Leicester: The British Psychological Society.

Steering Committee on Test Standards. (1994). *Certificate of Competence in Occupational Testing Level A: Guidance for Assessors – Second Edition.* Leicester: The British Psychological Society.

Steering Committee on Test Standards. (1996). *Psychological Testing: A User's Guide.* Leicester: The British Psychological Society.

Sutherland, S. (1994). *Irrationality: the enemy within.* Harmondsworth: Penguin.

Tyler, L. (1984). 'What tests don't measure'. *Journal of Counseling and Development, 63,* 48-50.

Glossary

Ability Literally, being able or having the power to do something. What a person can do on the basis of skill, expertness, knowledge or talent.

Achievement test A test of maximum performance designed to measure knowledge, learning or proficiency. Usually refers to tests designed to measure the outcomes of training or instruction.

Actuarial prediction A method of making decisions that is based on existing data from an expectancy table. A decision where judgement is not used.

Adaptive testing An approach to testing where the questions asked are determined by the replies given to earlier questions. It is used in computer-based testing to present individuals with items that are neither too easy nor too difficult.

Adverse impact A situation where some test takers find a test more difficult than others for reasons not related to the test's ability to predict subsequent performance.

Allocation See Placement.

Alternate form Another version of a test, either an equivalent one, or one designed for a different target population (e.g. for a different age group).

Aptitude test A test, usually of maximum performance, designed to predict future performance in a job, training programme, or similar activity.

Assessment centre A selection process which includes a variety of assessment exercises and where a group of applicants are assessed by a team of assessors. Exercises might include psychological tests, job simulations, group discussions, presentations and so on.

Attainment The level of performance achieved after appropriate training and practice.

Attenuation When scores on two variables are correlated, measurement error reduces the correlation coefficient obtained. Restriction in the range of scores will also reduce the correlation coefficient. This reduction is called attenuation. Formulae can be used to estimate the correlation coefficient that would have been obtained if there was no measurement error or the score range was not restricted.

Barnum effect The tendency of test reports to appear plausible and authoritative because of the way they are presented.

Base rate The proportion of people in the population under study who exhibit the characteristic being measured by the test.

Bias Systematic error in testing that affects some test takers more than others. It has the effect of enhancing or depressing the scores of some people taking the test. A concept that can apply to individual test items or to tests.

Certification The decision as to whether someone is qualified to a certain standard.

Classification The type of decision where someone is assigned to a category.

Concurrent validity An approach to test validation where a test is evaluated according to the extent to which test scores diagnose existing status or predict known criterion performance.

Confidence interval As test scores are estimates it is better to express them as score ranges. The 95% confidence interval refers to the score range within which we can be 95% certain that a person's score falls.

Constant error An error that affects all persons taking a test at a particular test session, or systematically affects a certain testing or measurement process.

Construct-related validity The analysis of the meaning of test scores in terms of the psychological concepts or 'constructs' that the test measures.

Content-related validity An approach to validity based on evaluating the representativeness of the test items for the purpose for which the test is designed.

Convergent validity Evidence of similarity between scores from a particular test and scores on other tests designed to measure the same construct.

Correlation A measure of the strength and direction of the relationship between two variables on a scale from −1.00 to +1.00 when scores are available for the same persons on both variables.

Criterion The standard against which predictions are judged. In selecting people for jobs, this might be a measure of job performance. In diagnosis, an independently derived judgement of the diagnosis usually based on expert judgement or more detailed assessment.

Criterion contamination A situation where measurement of the criterion is affected by knowledge of test performance.

Criterion-referenced An approach to scoring tests based on the behaviour to be expected from someone with a particular test score. Strictly defined it implies that test performance is used to specify the probability of certain behaviour, as in an expectancy table.

Criterion-related validity Approaches to validating a test where test scores are correlated with existing data or will be correlated with performance on the criterion (e.g. job performance) the test is designed to predict.

Cut-off score In selection, the score below which applicants are rejected. In screening, persons scoring above or below the cut-off score may be selected depending on circumstances.

Diagnosis A decision to allocate someone to a treatment category based on the existence of an explanation for their illness, dysfunction or distress.

Divergent validity Evidence that scores on a particular test are not related to scores on tests known to measure other unrelated constructs.

Domain-referenced An interpretation of a test score in terms of an estimate of level of ability; for example, can solve simple algebraic equations. Mainly used for interpreting test scores in education or training.

Effect size The difference between the scores of two groups expressed in units of standard deviation. Calculated by dividing the difference in scores by the standard deviation of the scores of the total sample.

Equivalence A process that is designed to generate scores that will be identical to those obtained from another measurement process. A parallel version of a test. Coefficient of equivalence is the correlation between two parallel tests.

Error of measurement The changes in test score found when the same test is taken a second time.

Expectancy table   A statistical table that summarizes the probability of different outcomes for persons who obtain particular test scores.

Face validity   The extent to which a test looks appropriate for its intended purpose, but not the extent to which it *is* appropriate.

Faking   When respondents adjust their replies to a questionnaire to try to create a false impression instead of replying honestly.

False negative   Person or persons predicted not to perform satisfactorily on the criterion measure who would have done so.

False positive   Person or persons predicted to perform satisfactorily on the criterion measure who do not do so. One type of error in prediction.

Forecasting efficiency   The percentage by which the use of a test reduces errors of prediction.

Hits   A term used to describe people whose criterion performance was correctly predicted by their test score.

Inter-individual   When comparisons are made between individuals.

Internal consistency   The extent to which items on a test, or from a particular scale of a test, associate with each other and with the total score on the test or scale.

Intra-individual   Within individual comparison, for example, when different test scores from the same individual are compared.

Inventory   A name frequently given to tests of typical response that measure personality or occupational interests.

Ipsative   A question format that aims to compare the relative preference of one individual for different activities, and not to compare the preferences of that individual with other people.

Item   A single question on a test.

Item bank   A set of items for a test. In computer-based testing, a large number of test items that have been classified by content and difficulty level.

Job analysis   The process of analysing what activities a particular job involves and how they contribute to successful job performance.

Maximum performance   How well someone can perform a task when making their best effort.

Mean   The arithmetical average of a set of scores.

Median   The middle score of a set of scores. The score at which half the people score above and half below.

Meta-analysis   The statistical method of cumulating the findings from many separate research studies to provide a more accurate estimate of the relationship between the test scores and the criterion.

Misses   A term used to describe people whose criterion performance was not predicted by their test scores.

Multivariate   Literally, many variables. A situation where many variables affect how an individual behaves.

Norm(s)   The set of scores obtained by a reference group with which an individual's test scores are being compared.

Normal distribution   The bell-shaped frequency distribution that is obtained from a long series of chance events. Many human attributes are distributed on a normal or near-normal distribution. The distribution of test scores often approximates a normal distribution.

Norm-referenced   When test scores are interpreted by comparison with the scores of a reference group.

Objectivity   The extent to which a test procedure or scoring process is independent of judgement on the part of the test administrator.

Peer rating   A rating of the performance of an individual or the description of the individual obtained from work colleagues, friends, relatives, etc.

Percentile   The way of expressing performance on a test in terms of the percentage of people taking the test or in a norm group who obtained scores below a particular individual.

Performance test A test of maximum performance involving actual performance of a task. A test of typical response where the test taker is observed in a standardized situation.

Placement Decisions where everybody is offered some kind of treatment. Sometimes called allocation.

Predictive validity An approach to test validation where a test is evaluated by the extent to which its scores predict future performance on the criterion.

Predictor The measure (e.g. test score) that is being used to predict performance on the criterion.

Profile A set of test scores for an individual, usually from the same test. Frequently presented in some form of graphical display to assist comparison between the different scores.

Projective techniques Tests where the subject is presented with a relatively unstructured task and is asked to provide an interpretation. Subjects are assumed to 'project' their feelings, beliefs, etc. in their replies.

Quartile The name given to the 25th and 75th percentiles. It is also the name given to the groups formed when a percentile distribution is divided into four equal parts.

Range The difference between two scores on a test. Frequently refers to the difference between highest and lowest scores. Also used to describe the upper and lower limits between which a person's test score probably falls.

Range restriction When the range of scores on a test is restricted because of lack of variability in a sample of test takers. Has the effect of reducing the observed correlation between test scores and other variables.

Rapport The degree of co-operation and communication between the test taker and the test administrator.

Raw score The direct numerical report of a person's performance on a test, or scale of a test; for example, the number of questions they got right on an ability test.

Reliability The degree to which test scores are free from errors of measurement.

Response set The tendency to answer questions in the same way regardless of item content.

Sample Some part of a larger body chosen to represent the whole. The process of doing this.

Scale A set of test items that have been demonstrated, or are assumed, to measure the same attribute (e.g. ability).

Scattergram The plot of individuals' scores on one variable against another. Frequently, the plot of individuals' scores on a test against their criterion performance or their scores on another test.

Screening An initial decision-making process to decide who to investigate further, e.g. shortlisting job applicants, many medical tests.

Selection The type of decision involving just two categories – acceptance and rejection.

Selection Ratio The proportion of those selected from the total population of candidates.

Self-report Information given by the test taker that is assumed to be descriptive of the test taker's typical behaviour.

Software author The person who develops the computer programs that administer, score and sometimes provide an interpretation of a test.

Spatial A test item that requires the test taker to work out whether an object or figure can be rotated or transformed in a certain way.

Specimen set One set of all the material for a test including the test manual, question booklet, answer sheet, scoring key, etc. It is designed to allow a potential test user to evaluate the test.

Stability The extent to which test scores remain the same over time or situations. The correlation between scores on the same test taken on two different occasions separated by a fixed time interval is used to measure stability.

Standard deviation A measure of the spread of a set of scores. The square root of the averaged squared deviation from the mean.

Standard error of measurement The standard deviation of the set of scores obtained from repeated measurement of the same person. Can be estimated if the reliability and variance of a set of scores are known.

Standardization Fixing the processes for administering a test (e.g. directions, scoring rules, etc). Sometimes also used to refer to the process of collecting data to establish norms for a test.

Standard score The number of standard deviations that a person's test score is above or below the mean. There are a number of standard score systems which define the mean and units for measuring standard deviation in such a way as to avoid negative scores.

State The present level of a psychological characteristic that varies according to the situation or time at which it is measured.

Style The characteristic way a person performs a task.

Systematic Describing something that is done in a methodical, orderly or planned way.

Systematic error A non-random error in measurement that affects all or some test takers.

Test A systematic procedure for observing behaviour and describing it using numerical scales or fixed categories.

Test administrator The person who actually supervises and has responsibility for test administration.

Test author The person who originally develops and researches the test.

Test catalogue The document produced by a test publisher that describes the tests they sell.

Test developer The person or group of people who develop, publish and market the test.

Test manual The document that describes in detail how a test should be used, its design and development, administration and scoring procedures. It should contain tables of norms, describe how the test was standardized and cite evidence for the reliability and validity of the test for the purposes for which it was designed.

Test publisher The organization that markets and distributes the test and its accompanying documentation.

Test reviewer The person who conducts a scholarly review to evaluate the suitability of the test for the uses proposed.

Test sponsor The person or organization that contracts for the development of the test or provision of a testing service.

Test taker The individual who takes a test.

Test user The person who requires the test results, normally for some decision-making purpose. A role that may be shared.

Trainability test A performance test that consists of an opportunity for the test taker to learn a task through demonstration and limited practice followed by an assessment of the test taker's performance on the task.

Trait The average state of an individual on a psychological construct. Sometimes assumed to be an enduring characteristic of the person that is possessed to some degree.

Treatment validity The extent to which the results from a test can be shown to be relevant to decisions about a person's treatment.

Typical response How a person will most probably react, think or feel in a given situation.

Utility analysis The technique for estimating the financial benefit from using a test for selecting people for jobs. It is based on estimates of how much productivity will be increased, and costing this.

Validation Investigation(s) required to justify the interpretation of test results.

Validity The extent to which the test measures what it is intended to measure. Evidence to justify the way a test has been developed and is used.

Validity generalization The hypothesis that results obtained from one predictive validity study would also be obtained when the same test is used in another situation with a similar criterion.

Variability How widely scores vary – see also Range.

Variable (noun) Technical term for a measure that may have a number of different values.

Variance The standard deviation squared.

Index